HAL LINDSEY

APOCALYPSE CODE

Library of Congress Cataloging-in-Publication Data

Lindsey, Hal 1929–

ISBN 1-888848-21-9

Library of Congress Catalog Card Number:
97-060814

Published by WESTERN FRONT LTD., Palos Verdes, CA.
Cover Design/Book Design/Typography: Karen Ryan
Printing: Banta, Menasha, WI
Manufactured in the United States of America

CONTENTS

WHY THE MEDIA CATASTROPHE CRAZE?

CHAPTER ONE

"I think human life is threatened as never before in the history of this planet. Not just by one peril, but by many perils that are all working together and coming to a head at about the same time. And that time lies close to the year 2000. I am one of those scientists who finds it hard to see how the human race is to bring itself much past the year 2000."

—Dr. George Wald
Nobel Prize-winning scientist, Harvard University

The movie wasn't an academy award contender by a long shot, yet I was amazed to see the audience's reaction. They sat both shocked and spellbound by the enormous destructive power of the natural disaster portrayed on the screen. The movie was *Dante's Peak*. It was about a volcano that erupted in the northwest part of the USA.

Time Magazine keyed on the movie and wrote a major article on the *"Volcanic Ring Of Fire"* that extends around the coastal regions of the continents and island chains that surround the Pacific Ocean. There are currently 550 active volcanos being monitored worldwide. Some—such as Mammoth Mountain in California, Popocatepetl near heavily populated Mexico City, and Mount Vesuvius near Naples and Sorrento, Italy—could erupt at any time and bring about hundreds of thousands of deaths. Remember, it was the eruption of Mount Vesuvius that destroyed Pompeii and all life around it in 79 AD. It was so terrible that it is still a symbol to this day of the tragic, uncontrollable power of an active volcano.

One very important factor to remember is that volcanos and *earthquakes* occur along the same fault lines and have an effect upon each other—sometimes triggering either an eruption or an earthquake.

Earthquakes have made media headlines in record numbers in recent years. There is a reason. They are increasing in frequency and destructiveness. In the decades since 1890 AD, earthquakes that caused great damage and loss of life remained fairly constant in number, averaging between 2 to 4—until the 1950s, that is. In the decade of the 1950s there were 9; in the decade of the 1960s, there were 13; in the decade of the 1970s there were 51; in the decade of the 1980s, there were 86; from 1990 through 1996, there have been more than 150. In fact, in 1996 alone, measuring by the Richter scale, there were 9 earthquakes in the 7 to 9 category, 56 in the 6 to 7 category, and 145 in the 5 to 6 range. It is very important to note the most damage caused last year was by earthquakes in the 5.6 to 6.5 range. This overrides the U.S. Geological Society's recent "reassessment" that only earthquakes of 7.0 should be considered "major" ones.

These are only a couple of the many global catastrophe themes that Hollywood, the television industry and national magazines have presented in the last five years.

TORNADOS MAKE THE BIG SCREEN

Twister was another popular disaster movie that depicted the horror of tornados and the fact that they are getting more powerful and frequent. It got the same type of audience response. Areas not previously hit by tornados in modern times are now experiencing this frightening demonstration of nature's random catastrophic power. Areas in Arkansas were hit with "twisters" of record-setting power and numbers in early March, 1997. They were then treated to record floods. One victim said, "It's like seeing the end of the world," as she looked over the devastation to her community.

EVIDENCE OF GLOBAL WARMING HEATS UP

The movie *Water World* vividly depicted what could (and some scientists believe will) happen as a result of global warming. I don't believe that there will be another universal flood. However, there could be a catastrophic rise in sea level. This would cause unimaginable consequences to the earth's oceanfront property, where the majority of the world's population lives.

Perhaps one of the worst impending catastrophes of all is the impending change in the earth's average temperatures with the consequent changes in global weather patterns. Scientists from many different fields have expressed great concern about mounting evidence that the world may be farther along in this menace than was first thought.

No one seems to know why the Planet is experiencing so many radical shifts in ecology in such a short period of time.

Some think it is being triggered by the enormous use of fossil fuels. Others feel it has something to do with the alarming damage that's been done to the ozone layer. As of the spring of 1997, the annual hole in the ozone layer has doubled. It is now computed to be twice the size of all of Europe. Animals in the southern part of Argentina have been found blind because of the effect of unfiltered sun rays on their eyes.

Still others believe it has resulted from the mindless destruction of spaceship earth's air purifiers—the rain forests. The truth is it's probably a combination of all these and other abuses we've heaped upon the Earth's ecosystems.

Evidences of a badly damaged ecology are showing up everywhere. From London, Reuters reported in 1994, "The British Antarctic Survey's Faraday Research Base on the Antarctic peninsula has recorded the fastest sustained warming since worldwide temperature records began 130 years ago. 'The rise is the fastest we have on record...People should be looking to the future or the consequences could be quite dire,' said Dr. John King, head of the survey's meteorological group."

The Associated Press reported from Buenos Aires in January, 1997, "A vast section of ice that is breaking away from the northern tip of Antarctica could make temperatures rise and speed up global flooding, a scientist warns. A chunk of ice measuring 48 miles by 22 miles has broken off the Larsen Ice Shelf. The iceberg was expected to drift north and melt in warmer water. Farther north, a 300-foot-deep ice shelf has collapsed, leaving only a plume of fragments in the Weddell Sea. The Larsen cracking was caused by regional warming that began in the 1940s and that scientists haven't been able to explain. The melting iceberg will make the climate warm up even faster while lowering ocean salt levels, geologist Rudolfo del Valle said in a telephone interview. He said that warming could have serious global effects. 'If conditions remain unchanged, this could cause catastrophic flooding all over the world,' he said."

Greenpeace, the international environmental group, gave a similar warning in a recent report:"*Entire island countries in the Pacific could disappear as sea levels rise and many plants and animals could face extinction as a result of the global warming.*" Scientists reported that great harbor cities like New York, Hamburg, Tokyo, Hong Kong, Sidney, Miami, San Francisco Bay cities, most of Holland, New Orleans, Bremen and Singapore, to name only a few, could cease to exist, under several feet of water. Most of the Earth's population centers are on oceanfronts.

THE COMING MONSTER STORMS

A corollary consequence of the global warming will be *storms of unprecedented destructive power*. Records set by severe weather and its aftermath are presently occurring all over the world. This is what is unique about the global weather pattern changes that are now taking place. Records in weather have routinely fallen in the past, but not all over the world, at the same time, and virtually every year.

Popular Science (Sept. 1995) ran a cover story on this theme entitled "HURRICANE ALERT: Killer Storms Are Coming". The article revealed, "A wave of killer hurricanes is long overdue, says the world's foremost hurricane expert, Colorado State University's weather wizard William Gray. . . In the longer run, the Delphic message from Fort Collins is one of impending calamity. Deeply disturbed by a vision of catastrophic disaster, Gray has been warning officials in charge of safety and preparedness about what lies ahead."

Typhoons, the Asian version of Hurricanes, are also increasing in record numbers and ferocity. As reported in *Earthweek: A Diary of the Planet,* recent Typhoons encountered at sea had sustained winds of over 230 miles per hour—an all-time record.

The average person is becoming increasingly apprehensive about the future as he is made aware of these catastrophes. I'm sure this is one of the reasons Hollywood has continued to increase production on this genre of film. Most everyone is interested to learn what might happen in the near future. There is almost a subliminal fear that something ominous and terrible is going to happen.

AND JUST WHEN YOU THOUGHT IT WAS SAFE TO COME OUT OF THE BOMB SHELTERS...

Asteroid was produced as a TV mini-series and drew a large audience. It portrayed in accurate scientific terms the kind of colossal catastrophe that would be caused by the collision of a metal-based asteroid with the earth. It also showed how helpless our technology is to divert such an object from a collision course toward earth.

A cover story in *Newsweek* (Nov. 23, 1992) titled *"Doomsday Science"* may have been the inspiration for this TV movie. Its lead paragraph declares, "Space is filled with objects that threaten Earth. Researchers are scrambling to ensure that worlds don't collide." According to Donald Yeomans of NASA's Jet Propulsion

Laboratory in Pasadena, California, "Earth runs its course about the sun *in a swarm of asteroids.* Sooner or later, our planet will be struck by one of them."

Is there really a possibility of an Apocalyptic collision of an asteroid or comet with Planet Earth? A review of past history coupled with new discoveries made possible by amazing new technologies now available to astronomers, physicists and geologists suggests there is high probability, possibly in the near future.

Using these new technologies, a group of scientists known as the Gehrels Group began some 20 years ago counting asteroids that orbit close enough to Earth to pose a threat. In the last few years of the 1980s they found an average of 15 per year that were large enough to wipe out all life on this planet. In 1992, the average asteroid count of this size rose to 35 per year. Now (1997), the count is up to just about 75 per year. In 1990 alone, Eleanor Helin of the Jet Propulsion Laboratory sighted 3 such asteroids in just four successive summer nights.

In 1992 a panel of NASA experts reported that there are between 1000 and 4000 asteroids crossing Earth's orbit that are bigger than a half mile across. Collision with any one of these would send civilization back to the stone age. They estimate that there are 300,000 Earth-crossing asteroids at least 300 feet across. Almost all of these chunks of rock and/or metal float between the orbits of Mars and Jupiter. The most frightening fact is that these asteroids frequently bump into each other like giant pinballs and are pushed into unpredictable orbits. Just such a "chance" occurrence could put an asteroid on collision course with Planet Earth and give us little warning of the approaching disaster.

Just how destructive can an asteroid be? Most scientists believe that an asteroid six miles across hit the earth in pre-history and destroyed the dinosaurs and most of all other life on the Earth. Some scientists calculated that if an asteroid the size of that "dinosaur asteroid" hit the Gulf of Mexico today, it would create a tidal wave 3 miles high. The tidal wave would still be at least 1,500 feet high after it traveled 900 miles. As far inland as Kansas City the wall of water would destroy everything. Even more scary, the impact would cause entire continents to burst into flames, set off numerous earthquakes with a magnitude over 8.0 on the Richter scale, block out sunlight—putting the earth into the equivalent of a so-called nuclear winter—and make agriculture globally impossible. Humans not destroyed in the initial collision would soon die. World ecology would be hopelessly damaged. Read on. This book will present some surprising predictions, and some shocking evidence that these sorts of things could happen soon.

REVENGE OF THE KILLER MICROBES

It was only 26 years ago that the U.S. Surgeon General declared the nation ready to "close the book on infectious diseases" as a thing of the past. A doctor friend of mine in 1969 told me not to write about the predictions of the Bible concerning worldwide plague. He said that modern medicine had virtually wiped out the possibility of plagues and other infectious diseases. "If you write that the Bible predicts *global plagues* as one of the signs of the end times," he warned, "you're going to discredit Bible prophecy and lose your own credibility." The book I was writing was called *The Late*

Great Planet Earth. Of course I did include the prediction of Jesus about the coming of great plagues, because I knew that we were at a point in the Biblical prophetic calendar when plagues would break out soon.

Today, as I knew it would, an entirely different reality has emerged. Mankind has never before faced such a threat from infectious diseases as we do now. And to make matters worse, many heretofore unknown, horrifying diseases have emerged—diseases like ebola, lyme disease, legionnaire's disease, flesh-eating bacteria, rift valley fever, dengue fever, and Hantaan virus.

Several major U.S. national magazines have published cover stories on these new health threats. *Popular Science* (Jan. 1996) did a cover story that declared, "Why We Are Losing The Fight Against DEADLY DISEASES." *Time* (Sept. 12, 1994) magazine's cover warned, "Revenge Of The KILLER MICROBES: Are we losing the war against infectious diseases?" The *Newsweek* (March 28, 1994) cover raised the question, "ANTIBIOTICS: The End of Miracle Drugs?"

Several bestselling books on this terrifying threat also appeared in the last few years, including *The Hot Zone* and *The Coming Plague* (non-fiction). *Virus,* a movie made for TV on this subject, scored high in the viewer ratings.

Hollywood noticed that the general population had a great concern about this subject, so they produced a major motion picture called "*Outbreak*". This made many people aware of one of the worst of the newly discovered diseases, the *Ebola Virus*. Ebola is almost 100% fatal. The infected victim dies in a gruesome way, bleeding from all orifices with their ravaged vital organs reduced to a liquid state.

AIDS, THE ULTIMATE PLAGUE

AIDS is arguably the worst plague that has ever hit the earth. Its long incubating period, known as the HIV Positive stage, usually results in many being infected by the carrier, often before the carrier even knows he or she is infected. Though it develops slowly, it is inevitably 100% fatal as of this writing. The thing that makes AIDS so difficult to fight is that it is primarily passed on through one of the human race's strongest drives—sex—thus guaranteeing its geometric spread.

When you factor in the fact that this is the first time in history a person infected with a 100% fatal infectious disease has been politically protected, there is no hope of ever stopping its spread. Even persons with the new strain of tuberculosis, which is not 100% fatal, are often quarantined. But it is illegal for a doctor to even tell his nurse that the person she is treating has AIDS. Many persons who have either HIV or full blown AIDS handle food in restaurants.

AIDS spread like wildfire in sub-Saharan Africa, where in many places it is reported that the average male has an average of 25 different sex partners per year. There are whole villages in this region where there are no more adults—only very old grandparents and very young children.

The Republic of South Africa has been viewed as the last hope for helping sub-Saharan Africa rise from its economic and social ruin. But recent medical reports from South Africa reveal a developing nightmare. Authorities estimate that there are at least 500,000 persons who are already HIV positive. Medical experts in the country indicate that the number of HIV carriers doubles every 13 months. They see brewing "a public health crisis of Apocalyptic proportions."

According to those consulted, they believe millions could die of AIDS in a relatively short time. They estimate that at the current rate of infection approximately 16 million South Africans between the ages of 14 and 50 could be HIV positive within five years.

To understand the catastrophic implications of this forecast, approximately 20 million South Africans voted in the recent general election. This means that most of the productive adult voters will soon be dead. The CIA is of the opinion that once 20% of the sexually-active population is HIV positive, the social structure collapses. This is exactly what happened in Zambia, Uganda and Zaire as reported in *The International Intelligence Briefing* on June 10, 1994.

SOME GRIM FACTS ABOUT AIDS

Here are the grim statistics of the known HIV/AIDS cases compiled by The World Health Organization (WHO) as of 1996:

HIV infected	29,400,000
AIDS cases	8,400,000
Deaths caused by AIDS	6,400,000

The epicenter of AIDS has shifted from Africa to the exploding populations of Asia. World health experts project that India alone, with the second largest population in the world, could have 50,000,000 infected with HIV by 2000 AD. In places like Bangkok, Thailand and Manilla, Philippines, which are world-renowned for female and male prostitution, the AIDS problem is already approaching catastrophic proportions. There has been a lucrative travel business in sex tours brought over from Europe and the U.S.A. for years (*Newsweek*, March 28, 1994).

AND NOW...THE END OF MIRACLE DRUGS?

At the beginning of the 1950s medical optimism was very high as so-called miracle drugs like penicillin and antibiotics became widely used, producing amazing results. Also there began to be great strides in the field of immunology and vaccines. It truly did appear that infectious diseases were on the verge of being wiped out.

But doctors like Richard Wenzel of the University of Iowa have soberly recognized that from the beginning of the miracle drugs, "man and microbe have been in a footrace. It's a race in which the lead keeps changing. In 1946, just five years after penicillin came into wide use with World War II, doctors discovered that staphylococcus had become invulnerable to the drug. No problem—smart pharmacologists invented or discovered new antibiotics. The drugs pounded the microbes into submission once again. But the bacteria regrouped, and mutants capable of fending off the latest drugs appeared. New drugs, newer mutants. And so it went. Overall, the drugs retained a slight lead and, slowly, scourges such as tuberculosis, bacterial pneumonia, blood poisoning, syphilis, gonorrhea and other bacterial infections that hark back to a time of high-button shoes were vanquished."

THE DEVILS OF THE MICROBE WORLD

Now, in 1997, we realize that the medical profession declared victory over the microbes unwisely, far too soon. "Bacteria are 'clever little devils' in ways that scientists never suspected," warns microbiologist Stanley

Falkow of Stanford University. They can develop immunity to one antibiotic and use its DNA code to develop resistance to another antibiotic they've not yet encountered (*Newsweek*, March 28, 1994).

Dr. Stuart Levy of Tufts University expressed his amazement at the way bacteria continually develop immunity to each new antibiotic introduced. In his book *Antibiotics Paradox*, he warns, "*The rise of drug-resistant germs is unparalleled in recorded biologic history.*"

How did bacteria finally snatch back the lead in their race against the human race and antibiotics? And after decades of the medical profession holding the lead, how did the microbes race ahead so quickly?

Certainly one of the first reasons resulted from the overconfidence of the medical field in declaring infectious diseases vanquished. Many of the major pharmaceutical companies shut down their research and pursuit of new antibiotics and looked for other medicines that had a more promising future profitability. Now it could take years to refocus and start up the antibiotic research again. By then, there could already be several pandemics of super-strain diseases that have already acquired drug resistance. Even though mankind quit making new weapons for the microbe war, microbes continued to rapidly develop immunity to our last line of defense.

Another reason was the over-prescribing of antibiotics by doctors. Many simple ailments would have better been treated with rest and proper nutrition supplemented with vitamins. Antibiotics should never have been prescribed for viral infections against which they were useless. With every prescription, we lessened the effectiveness of antibiotics for the future.

Another reason was that many patients quit taking the prescribed course of antibiotics as soon as they felt better. As a result, the particular bacterium that caused the illness was never destroyed, thus being left free to seize the antibiotic's DNA code and develop immunity to it. "As part of this drug resistance process, disease organisms are constantly swapping genes with each other, so mutations that bring drug resistance occur. *There's more genetic engineering taking place in your intestine than in all of the biotechnology companies,'* says microbiologist Barry Bloom of the Albert Einstein College of Medicine in New York City" (*Popular Science,* Jan. 1996).

One of the main reasons for bacteria's victory is the enormous overuse of antibiotics by farmers seeking to increase production and profit from livestock. The U.S. Food and Drug Administration is supposed to regulate and limit the number and amount of some 80 antibiotics that are approved for use with farm animals. But when the General Accounting Office of the U.S. Congress did their own check of milk from several locations, they found *traces of as many as 64 antibiotics at levels that raise health concerns, that is, they could produce resistant germs in milk drinkers.* Abuses have also been found in beef, chicken and lamb production. These constant low doses helped bacteria to develop resistance to them.

Rutgers University did a study recently that found a direct cause and effect relationship between the use of antibiotics deemed safe by the FDA and new strains of drug-resistant bacteria. The rate of increase at which drug-resistant bacteria developed found by this study was between 600% to 2700% (*Popular Science,* Jan. 1996).

THE AGE OF SUPER-INFECTIOUS DISEASES

Today we are in a battle that is much more grim than before the advent of the miracle drugs. The simple fact is that we now have super strains of mankind's old nemeses that have developed immunity to virtually all known drugs. They are storming back almost like they were out for revenge. Now the infectious disease threat is much more dangerous than before because they've developed immunity to most all antibiotics and they are much stronger. Thanks to the marvel of modern jet aircraft, there is now a transportation system that can spread these new super diseases around the world in a few days—super strains of tuberculosis, cholera, yellow fever, dengue fever, malaria. The World Health Organization (WHO) estimates that someone dies of malaria every 15 seconds.

"Merck & Co. views drug-resistant bacteria as a threat every bit as serious as the AIDS epidemic and is attacking them with the same fervor, says Bennet M. Shapiro, a top research executive at Merck. Yet he and others concede that it may take years for new breakthrough drugs to hit the market" (*Wall Street Journal,* July 1, 1996).

AN URGENT WARNING FROM WHO

WHO warned in 1995 that "*the world is ripe for super plagues of apocalyptic proportions.*" In 1996, WHO Director-General Dr. Hiroshi Nakajima warned, "We are standing on the brink of a global crisis in infectious diseases. The optimism of a relatively few years ago that many of these diseases could be brought under control has led to a fatal complacency. This complacency is now costing millions of lives."

"During the past 20 years, at least 30 new diseases have emerged to threaten the health of hundreds of millions of people. For many of these diseases there is no treatment, cure or vaccine... Diseases that have been around for centuries are popping up in incurable strains," said the WHO report.

The explosion of drug-resistant, super-strain diseases; the fact that a great part of the world population is undernourished, living with abominable sanitation and medical care that is poor or none at all; and the ability of infected people to travel to all parts of the world within hours—all contribute to catastrophes of the magnitude of those found in Bible prophecies about the Last Days.

THE SUM OF CATASTROPHE IS OVERWHELMING

Global warming, rising sea levels, weather pattern changes, monster storms, increasing numbers of earthquakes, volcanic eruptions, plagues, super strains of old diseases, the demise of 'miracles drugs,' tornados, famines, floods, killer heat waves, killer cold waves, and the like, are driving many to search for clues as to where it's all leading. No wonder their is another boom...

THE PSYCHIC BOOM

Along with the scientists, psychics and prophets of many persuasions predict an assortment of soon-coming global catastrophes for Planet Earth. Whether it's

Nostradamus, Edgar Casey, astrologers, palmists, Satanists, fortune tellers, or New Age prophets, to name a few, all have forecast some of these things.

However, the prophets of the Bible also foresaw these approaching catastrophes—only they predicted them two to three thousand years ago. With their unerring historical record of fulfillment, I belief it is important to listen at this moment in history to the greatest of these prophets, Jesus himself. When He was asked for signs of His second coming, He predicted there would be global catastrophes like **birthpains** in a woman about to give birth shortly before the time for His return. In other words, all the predicted signs would increase in frequency and intensity within the same time frame—shortly before His coming. He concluded His prophecy by applying it with this parable. This a summary of it: Just as we can tell that the general time of summer is near when see the first leaves on the fig tree, so we will be able to tell the general time of His return when we see all the prophecies of His return coming together and increasing in frequency and intensity. He said that the general time would be this: the generation that sees the prophecies come together in concert will live to see their final fulfillment (see Matthew 24:32-34).

Here is a description of those **birthpains** Jesus predicted would occur shortly before his return: **"Then He continued by saying, 'Ethnic group will rise against ethnic group, and kingdom against kingdom, and there will be great earthquakes, and in various places plagues and famines; and there will be terrors and great unprecedented signs from heaven [outer space]... And there will be extraordinary signs [shmeia]* in the sun and**

---

*Bauer, Arndt and Gingrich, σημεια "A miracle that is a sign of some greater meaning."

moon and stars, and upon the earth dismay among nations, in perplexity at the roaring of the sea and the waves, men fainting [literally "to stop breathing and die"] **from fear and the expectation** [extreme anxiety] **of things which are coming upon the world, for the powers of the heavens** [atmosphere, solar system and galaxies] **will be shaken"** (Luke 21:10–11, 25–26 HL).

The word **"shaken"**, which is σαλευθησο‍σται in the original Greek text, is presented as the real source of the unprecedented fear and anxiety that cause a great number of people to drop dead. As used here, it means that the perceived laws of astrophysics will waver throughout the observable universe. The things we have always taken for granted, like the stars, planets, solar systems and galaxies continuing on exact orbits with exact timing, will waver from their usual orbits and timing. It will appear that the whole universe is going to spin out of control. Mankind will be forced to ponder the question, "What or Who holds the Universe in place?" The fact that the verb is in the passive voice emphasizes that all this terrifying disruption of the universe is from an outside source that is far greater in power than any innate power within the natural, tangible universe itself. In other words, it faces mankind with an undeniable fact that Aristotle observed centuries ago—"There is an Unmoved Mover behind the Universe that is far greater than the Universe." It took someone infinitely greater than the universe to create it. The challenge is thrown down to man in a very simple statement:

"In beginning the Word had always existed; and the Word has always been face to face with

God; and as to His nature, the Word has always been God... All things came into being through Him, and apart from Him nothing came into being that ever has come into being... And the Word became flesh and dwelt among us, and we beheld His glory, glory as of the only begotten One from the Father, full of grace and truth" (John 1:1, 3, 14 HL).

Whatever one thinks about the Bible, I believe it is rather obvious that things predicted in the first century AD or earlier are in clear view today. One would be hard pressed not to recognize this in view of the media attention given to the very phenomena the prophets predicted... So read on, and discover more shocking things that are coming soon. And most important, you may find out a way to escape the worst of it.

THE
APOCALYPSE
CODE

CHAPTER TWO

"About the time of the end, a body of men will be raised up who will turn their attention to the prophecies of the Bible, and insist on their literal interpretation in the midst of much clamor and opposition."

—Sir Isaac Newton (AD 1643–1727)

There are many sources of prophecy today. As noted in the last chapter, there are extraordinary reasons for people to seek some sort of understanding of the future. Some are quite amazing in that they have been correct as much as 60% of the time.

However, what John the Apostle foresaw nearly 2000 years ago has more to do with this generation's immediate future than tomorrow's breaking news on CNN.

THE OLD TIGER
WHO WOULDN'T QUIT

He was in the least likely place and situation for such a revelation. John was a prisoner of Rome on the remote desert island penal colony of Patmos in the Aegean Sea off the coast of what is now Turkey. He was about 92 years old at the time, yet he had such a bold faith that he defied the Roman magistrate's order to no longer proclaim Jesus as Messiah, Savior and Lord. The Roman Governor did not want to execute him, for he feared his martyrdom would spread Christianity even more rapidly. So instead, he sent John to the notorious penal colony on the island of Patmos to die of "natural causes." There he was thrown in with violent criminals to fend for himself. But John simply won many of the criminals to faith in Jesus. They then became his disciples and protectors. And to the dismay of the Roman rulers, he continued to survive.

It was there, under extremely difficult conditions, where John wrote down in a scroll all that "he **saw** and **heard**" during what must have been an experience of *time travel* to the beginning of the 21st century.

The Book of Revelation in the English Bible should properly be called *The Apocalypse*, which is the Greek word at the beginning of its first sentence. This word actually describes the book's purpose. For most, *The Apocalypse* has been an intriguing enigma and inscrutable mystery for centuries. Many scholars of all Christian denominations have either marvelled over it, scoffed at it or allegorized its prophetic content into absurd historical allegories about the early Christian era. They see its message as already fulfilled, not prophetic and not very important. It has rarely been taught in most mainline denominations.

THE MODERN PROPHECY MOVEMENT BEGINS

In this generation there is another reality developing. The appearance of many books that made Bible prophecy understandable to the common man, starting with *The Late Great Planet Earth* in May of 1970, has caused a demand for teaching on the subject. This unprecedented interest by the average Christian in Bible prophecy in general and the Apocalypse in particular is driving ministers of all persuasions back to their studies. As a result, it is being examined by both friend and foe with a new interest—by the former to explain it better, by the latter to explain it away. I rejoice that at least it is being studied.

The most amazing research in connection with the Apocalypse, however, has been done by a line of Biblical scholars who down through the centuries took the Apocalypse seriously and sought to understand its message in the most literal futuristic sense possible. This group, from many different denominations, sees its primary message as prophetic to the events that occur just before, during and after the Second Coming of the Messiah, Jesus of Nazareth. While seeking to understand the other views, I have studied continuously to understand this unique book, with all of its challenges, for over forty years.

HOW THE APOCALYPSE WAS REVEALED TO JOHN

A careful study of the Apocalypse suggests that the writer used certain composite descriptions taken from his worldview, which was shaped by his understanding of what existed in the first century AD. He was forced to do this because of the extraordinary manner the message was revealed to him.

The Apostle John's sworn testimony about how he received the messages is given in the first chapter: **"The unveiling of hidden things (αποκαλυψις) concerning Jesus Christ, which GOD gave Him to show His servants, even the hidden things which must soon take place; and He sent His personal Angel to communicate it to His servant John, who bore careful witness to everything he saw— that is, about the Word of GOD and the testimony concerning Jesus Christ. Blessed is the one who reads the words of this PROPHECY, and blessed are those who hear it and take to heart what is written in it, because the time is near"** (Revelation 1:1-3 HLL).

No other book in the Bible so carefully and fully explains its supernatural origin, its chain of transmission, and the exact way the message was communicated to the writer. It also stresses that John was commanded to write *about only the things to which he was a personal eyewitness.*

In translating the first three verses from the original Greek, I gave special attention to the word, αποκαλυψις, from which the book gets its name. Concerning its meaning when used in a prophetic context, one of the world's best authorities writes, "When used in the eschatological (prophetic) sense it means *'the disclosure of secrets belonging to the last days'.*"* The meaning of this word had a big impact on me when I related it to Daniel's very important similar personal statement at the end of his book of prophecy

*Bauer, Walter, as Revised and Augmented by F. W. Gingrich and Frederick Danker; *A Greek-English Lexicon Of The New Testament And Other Early Christian Literature.*

(Daniel 12:4-8). I will go into this personal revelation in a moment.

I also sought to bring out another fine, but important, point of Greek grammar in establishing the relationship of αποκαλυψις to Jesus Christ. The genitive case is used, and it can have either an objective or a subjective meaning. Now I know you're probably thinking, "Who cares about the old boring Greek grammar?" But its meaning here is imperative to the understanding of the book. If it is objective, then it means "the unveiling of secrets *that belong* to Jesus Christ." If it is subjective, it means "the unveiling of prophetic secrets *concerning or about* Jesus Christ." The subjective sense actually explains the purpose of the whole book, because the very essence of the Apocalypse is to reveal or unveil the secret prophetic things that center not only in who Jesus Christ really is, but in what He is going to do with Planet Earth.

DISCOVERING THE APOCALYPSE CODE

When I fully grasped that John was to write only about things he had actually seen, I traced through the whole Book of the Apocalypse to confirm whether the insight was correct.

For instance, in chapter one, verses 10 and 11, John wrote, "...I *heard* behind me a loud voice like a trumpet, which said: '*Write* on a scroll *what you see...*' " And in verse 19, "...Write, therefore, the things *you have seen*, even the things which are, and the things which shall take place after these things."

In chapter four, verse 1, "After these things, *I looked*, and behold a door standing open in heaven, and the first voice which *I heard*, like the sound of a trumpet speaking with me, said, 'Come up here, and *I will show you what must take place after these things.*"

The essential point is this: John constantly testifies throughout the Book that he "saw" and "heard" the things about which he writes.

THE GREAT DIVIDE OF PRESENT AND FUTURE HISTORY

As is true of the Apostle John's writing style in his other books, he gives a general outline of the Apocalypse's message. Verse 19 quoted above gives the plot point that clearly informs us when the message switches from the events of this present age, in which God is dealing with the world through the Gentile-dominated Church, to the resumption of an interrupted age, in which God dealt with the world through the Israelites. The divine spotlight is shifted to Israel and Jerusalem again from chapters six through nineteen.

So John was commanded to write about the things to which he was an eyewitness. First, he is to write about **"even the things which are..."**, which refers to our present age, and second, about **"the things which shall take place after these things"**, which refers to things that take place *after* the present age.

The original words for **"after these things"** are "meta tauta." These exact same words are used at the beginning of chapter four, where there is an obvious plot point change to future things that happen within a period of seven years and an approximate six months prelude, climaxing with the Second Coming of Jesus, the Messiah. The imperative point to note is that John is declared an "eyewitness" to the prophecies of both periods.

JOHN'S TIME TRAVEL EXPERIENCE

This was the question I pondered over and prayed about for a long time—How could John be an 'eyewitness' to events of the 20th and 21st centuries? Just exactly how would a first century prophet describe, much less understand, the incredible advances in science and technology that exist at the end of the 20th and the beginning of the 21st centuries? Yet, he testified and God bore witness that he actually saw and heard things like:

- supersonic jet aircraft with missiles, hyperspeed cannons, guided bombs
- advanced attack helicopters
- modern main battle tanks
- intercontinental ballistic missiles with Multiple Independently Targeted Reentry Vehicles tipped with thermonuclear warheads (ICBMs that are MIRVed).
- battlefield artillery and missiles with neutron-nuclear warheads
- biological and chemical weapons
- aircraft carriers, missile cruisers, nuclear submarines
- laser weapons
- space stations and satellites
- the new super secret HAARP weapon system (High-frequency Active Auroral Research Program)

that can change weather patterns over whole continents, jam global communications systems, disrupt human mental processes, manipulate the earth's upper atmosphere, etc.

TALK ABOUT FUTURE SHOCK...

Now this is only a partial list, but it does illustrate the point. I believe that the Spirit of God gave me a special insight, not only into how John described what he actually experienced, but also into how this whole phenomenon encoded the prophecies so that they could be fully understood only when their fulfillment drew near.

Picture yourself in John's place for a moment. Suppose you are miraculously transported from the primitive, non-technical age of the 1st century up to the 21st century. You witness the most horrific war of all times, fought with machines completely beyond your comprehension. Then you are given a divine command to describe accurately in writing what you saw, heard and felt. *Star Wars,* with all of its futuristic projections, can't even begin to approximate the leap forward in science that John experienced.

THE GREAT TIME WARP

This is the essence of what I have come to call the Apocalyptic Code. John had to describe in terms of his 1st century knowledge what he saw. The encoded prophecies can be understood only when we prayerfully seek to decipher what in today's vast arsenal of technical marvels fits best John's 1st century description of them.

A CONFIRMING REVELATION

I prayerfully sought for a confirmation of my *apocalyptic code* theory in some other prophetic passages in the Bible. One day while studying the Prophet Daniel for the umpteenth time, I was startled by a thought that came to mind while analyzing a familiar passage. Daniel received the prophecy I was studying at the end of his prophetic writing career. He had just received a long extraordinary prophecy that gave vital information about: the future rise of the Jewish False Prophet and his cohort known as the Antichrist of Rome; the battle plan and stages of escalation of the world's final great war; and the rescue of a believing remnant of Israelis and their future destination.

After such an experience, and I'm sure he remembered all of the previous prophecies of world-shaking events, he was overwhelmed and mystified. He did not understand the things that he himself had been directed to write. So he prayed for a divine interpretation of the meaning of it all. This is part of the answer given to him: **"But as for you Daniel, *shut up* [encode] the words and *seal* the scroll UNTIL the *time of the end;* many shall run to and fro [in search of its meaning], and [general] knowledge shall increase."** ..."**Although I heard, I did not understand. Then I said, 'My Lord, what shall be the end of these things?' And he said, 'Go your way, Daniel, for the words are *closed up* and *sealed* TILL the *time of the end.* Many shall be purified, and made white, and refined, but the wicked shall get more wicked; and none of the wicked shall understand, but *the wise shall understand*"** (Daniel 12:4, 8-10 NKJV).

As I thought about the idea of closing up and sealing the book of prophecy until the time of the end, which is the time just before the coming of the Messiah Jesus, it hit me. All that is to be written in prophecy about the end times has already been written. So if the prophecies are shut up and sealed, it must be by encoding the message until the time for it to be understood arrives.

HOW WAS PROPHECY ENCODED

Careful students of the Apocalypse have known for centuries that there was a special encoding of certain parts of the book. This was done by a system of carefully developed symbols used in many parts of the Bible. As we will see in detail in chapter seventeen, there are certain symbols used to describe Rome and a religious system closely associated with it. The term **Mystery Babylon** is used to describe an aspect of Rome, which if written clearly without encoding, would have been mistakenly understood by Caesar as an attack of Christians on his divinity and the Empire. This would have resulted in an all-out slaughter of Christians throughout the Empire.

The term **whore of Babylon** is said to cause **the kings of the earth to commit adultery with her**. Again, Spirit-led students of the Bible know that when the context indicates these terms are being used in a symbolic sense, they always have a consistent meaning. For instance, when **adultery** is used symbolically, it almost always means spiritual infidelity with a false religion. In the same way, **whore** is consistently used to mean a counterfeit religion.

Sometimes in the Apocalypse things are tightly reasoned and the symbols are explained within the same chapter. For instance, it is amazing how many times I studied Apocalypse, chapter 17, before it was revealed to me just who **the woman,** who is **the whore,** really is. Yet it is clearly explained in the same chapter with this explanation, **"And the woman whom you saw is the great city, which *is reigning* over the kings of the earth"** (Rev. 17:18 NASB). The present tense is used with the verbal construction for **"to reign."** The root idea of the Greek present tense verb is "continuous action in the present time." So the idea stressed in this identification is that "the **woman** who is also called the **whore** with the inscription written on her forehead, **'Mystery Babylon the Great' (Revelation 17:5)**—is none other than the city of ROME. Only Rome fits this encoded description at the time the Apostle John wrote this book.

You see, the interpretation was there all the time. But it was encoded so that only a Christian guided by the Spirit of God would be able to interpret it. And, as Daniel predicted, the Scroll of Prophecy was sealed until the last days. This kind of encryption is frequently used in the Apocalypse and certain other places in the Bible. You may well be asking—Why so much in the Apocalypse?

One good reason God inspired John to use these *encrypted Biblical symbols* is obvious. Had John clearly revealed some of the things he wrote in the Apocalypse that were against the Roman Empire (even though he was referring to its revived form of the last days), the Roman government—not understanding that this referred to a future revived form of the old Roman Empire—would have branded this a seditious book that plotted the overthrow of the Empire. As a result, all Christians in the empire would've been arrested and executed without mercy.

THE APOCALYPSE CODE AND THE THIRD MILLENNIUM

But even though so many of the encoded symbols in the book are explained either in the context, in another part of the book of the Apocalypse, or in other books of the Bible, there were others that had no Biblical parallel whatsoever. This is why the Apocalypse code explained earlier is so important. The unique concept of a "first century time traveler" accelerated up to the beginning of the 21st century; of being vividly shown all the phenomena of a global war fought with weapons of unimaginable power, speed and lethality; of being brought back to the first century and told to write an accurate eyewitness account of this terrifying future time—is the essence of understanding his code.

Let me give one illustration—the rest will be interpreted as they are encountered in the Apocalypse. These strange encoded symbols describe a creature that never existed in nature:

"The locusts *looked like* horses prepared for battle. On their heads they wore *something like* crowns of gold, and their faces *resembled* human faces. Their hair was *like* women's hair, and their teeth were *like* lions' teeth. They had breastplates of iron, and the sound of their wings was *like* the thundering of many horses and chariots rushing into battle. They had tails and stings like scorpions, and in their tails they had power to torment people for five months" (The Apocalypse 9:7-10).

Note that John keeps saying, **"looked like, something like, resembled, was like, etc."** By these qualifying terms, John sought to emphasize that he was aware of describing vehicles and phenomena far beyond his first century comprehension. So he used symbols drawn from 1st century phenomena that "looked like" these marvels of science. Using a mixed composite of things from the 1st century, he strove to represent what he saw.

With that in mind, let's see if we can find the passage's meaning. The vehicle's overall shape looked to John like a **"locust."** The general outer shape of a helicopter is similar to that of a locust.

The phrase **"horses prepared for battle"** probably means "the attack helicopters" were heavily armored. John had seen Romans drape armor over their horses to protect them from arrows, lances and swords.

At this point John seems to switch to what he saw inside the machine. The phrase **"something like crowns of gold"** most likely describes the elaborate helmets worn by helicopter pilots. And **"their faces resembled human faces. . ."**—as John looked at the front of the helicopter, the face of the pilot appeared through the front windscreen. The appearance of something that looked like **a woman's hair** could describe the whirling propeller that looked like filmy hair. Remember, John had never seen a large instrument spinning so fast that it couldn't be seen clearly. The term **"teeth"** probably describes the weaponry projecting from the "chopper"—there is a monster six-barrel cannon suspended from the nose of most attack helicopters today. The **"sound of the their wings was like many horses and chariots rushing to battle"**—those of us who have heard the thunderous sound of many military helicopters flying overhead can relate to this description. Vietnam veterans have vivid memories of the constant thundering of helicopter engines and the thumping noise of the main rotor blades. In fact, the helicopter and its noises became a virtual symbol of the Vietnam War.

Today, helicopters such as the Apache, Cobra, and Comanche have become an essential, integral part of the army's mobile equipment. They are used as lethal tank killers, reconnaissance gatherers, rapid haulers of equipment and re-enforcement troops for insertion into critical areas, as artillery destroyers, interceptors of enemy helicopters, rocket launchers against massed enemy troops, for insertion of special elite troops behind enemy lines, as rescue ambulances for the critically wounded, etc.

This is just a sample of the kind of descriptions John recorded in this mysterious book of prophecy. It is my belief that current events and technology can give us insights into the amazing Book of the Apocalypse that couldn't have been discerned in other generations. This is the encoding that had to be unlocked by discerning the symbols which describe weapons and phenomena in the light of current science and technology. This is the code that most effectively kept prophecy concealed until the time of the end. I am convinced that time is now!

GATHERING THE CODES

To summarize, many symbols used in the Apocalypse are interpreted for us by explanations given within their own context. Others are explained in some parallel passages in other books of the Bible. But there are some symbols that have no Biblical explanation. These are the ones that have been a mystery to interpreters through the centuries. All of these symbols helped to so encode the message that only a spiritually alive person guided by the Spirit of God has been able to unlock its prophetic content. The code-symbols that have no Biblical parallel or interpretation couldn't be understood until the time of their fulfillment drew near.

So get ready for a grand adventure as we seek to unlock many prophecies couched in these coded symbols. I believe they will combine to show that we are very near the time of their fulfillment—that time about which Jesus predicted, **"...unless those days were cut short, no living thing would be left alive."**

CHAPTER THREE

TRUE PROPHETS CAN'T BE GUESSERS

CHAPTER THREE

"Surely the Sovereign LORD
does nothing without revealing his plan
to his servants the prophets."

—Amos 3:7 NIV

As the old saying goes, "Coming close counts in tossing horseshoes and hand grenades." But coming close isn't good enough to qualify as a true Biblical prophet. Either the prophecies were bullseyes, or the prophet was destined to become a rock pile. The prophet who proved to be false was stoned to death under the direct command of the Law of Moses.

Moses, the greatest prophet of the Hebrew Bible, was the first to write down his prophecies. Thus near the end of his life he received a command from the God he served to instruct all who followed after as to how to discern a true prophet from a false prophet.

FALSE PROPHETS' SOURCE IS SUPERNATURAL BUT DANGEROUS

Moses declared, **"For those nations, which you shall dispossess, listen to those who practice witchcraft and to diviners, but as for you, the LORD your God has not allowed you to do so. The LORD your God will raise up for you a prophet like me from among you, from your countrymen, you shall listen to him"** (Deuteronomy 18:14-15 NASB).

Moses knew the people would need prophets to reveal relevant things about the future and to give direction from God, especially in times of great stress. God, through Moses, commands them not to go to prophets who get their message from the various forms of the occult. But they were to listen to only the Israelite He chose to be His prophet. Nothing was more catastrophic for the Israelite than to receive a false prophecy and then to act on the wrong information. God warns them that the reason he judged the nations that were there before them was because they sought to know the future by means of the occult.

HOW TO KNOW A TRUE PROPHET

Naturally, God anticipated what the people would ask about this prophet to whom they were to listen and obey. God said through Moses, **"And it shall come about that whoever will not listen to My words which he shall speak in My name, I Myself** will require it of him. **But the prophet who shall speak a word presumptuously in My Name which I have not commanded him to speak, or which he shall speak in the name of other gods, THAT PROPHET SHALL DIE.**

"**And you may say in your heart, 'How shall we know the word which the LORD has not spoken?' When a prophet speaks in the name of the LORD, IF THE THING DOES NOT COME ABOUT OR COME TRUE, that is the thing which the LORD has not spoken. The prophet has spoken it presumptuously; you shall not be afraid of him**" (Deuteronomy 18:20-22 NASB).

This teaches us that the true prophet had to predict some things that would take place in his lifetime so that his authenticity could be verified. He had to also be specific enough that his prophecies couldn't be manipulated by man. But if a prophecy he declared in the name of the LORD did not come true, he was to be executed by stoning, which was commanded by the Law of Moses.

ISAIAH'S CHALLENGE TO FALSE PROPHETS

The Prophets of Israel were very aware of this test. In the following quote, God confirmed Isaiah as a true Prophet, and at the same time condemned the false prophets whose source was the occult. " **'Present your case,' the LORD God says** (to the fortune tellers.) **'Bring forward your strong arguments,' The King of Jacob says. Let them bring forth and declare to us what** *is going to take place*; **As for** the former events, declare what they were, that we may consider them, and know their outcome; Or announce to us *what is coming.* Declare the things that *are going to come afterward, so that we may know that you are gods*; Indeed, do good or evil, that we may anxiously look about us and fear together" (Isaiah 41:21-23 NASB).

The LORD threw down the gauntlet to these false prophets. His challenge was centered in the taunts, **"...declare to us what is going to take place,"** and, **"...Announce to us what is coming. Declare the things that are going to come afterward, so that we may know you are Gods..."** The challenge to these false prophets is for them to predict 100% accurately the things that are coming in the future.

Here is the truly startling thing; the LORD declares flatly that if they can make specific predictions without error, then they will prove themselves to be Gods. Why? Because only God can predict the future in specifics without error. Even the best of the secular prophets can't boast of an accuracy of more than 60%. Speaking through Isaiah again, the LORD makes this clear:

"'I, the LORD, am the maker of all things, Stretching out the heavens by Myself, And spreading out the earth all alone, *Causing the omens of boasters to fail, Making fools out of diviners, Causing wise men to draw back,* **And turning their knowledge into foolishness,** *Confirming the word of His servant,* **And performing the purpose of His messengers...'"** (Isaiah 44:24-26 NASB).

Here are some illustrations from history of how

the Prophets of the LORD, who were all guided directly by the Spirit of GOD, made prophecies that validated within their lifetime that they were true Prophets by the test given by Moses.

THE CASE OF MICAIAH: ONE MAN AND GOD ARE A MAJORITY

This is about an incident in which the Godly King Jehoshaphat of Judea (the southern kingdom of the three tribes of Judah, Benjamin and Levi), who was a true believer in the LORD, was influenced by the evil, non-believing King Ahab of Israel (the northern kingdom of the other ten tribes).

Ahab had been irreversibly corrupted by his pagan Sidonian wife, Jezebel, who was devoted to the awful demonic deity named Baal. This is the one to whom Israelites sacrificed their children. She brought to Israel with her 400 prophet-priests of Baal.

In this atmosphere, Ahab invited King Jehoshaphat down to Samaria for a state visit. Ahab threw a lavish banquet for Jehoshapahat and poured upon him many flattering honors. Then he seduced him into joining with him in an attack against Ramoth Gilead.

But God's Spirit prompted Jehoshapat to insist, **"Let us first seek the counsel of the LORD"** (II Chronicles 18:4). So Ahab cleverly slipped in Jezebel's 400 prophets and asked them, **"Shall we go to war against Ramoth Gilead, or shall I refrain?"** The false prophets predictably answered, **"Go, for God will give it into the king's hand."**

But Jehoshapat did not accept these prophecies and asked, **"Is there not a prophet of the LORD** here from whom we may inquire?" **The king of Israel answered Jehoshaphat, "There is still one man through whom we can inquire of the LORD, but I hate him because he never prophesies anything good about me, but always bad. He is Micaiah, son of Imlah"** (Micaiah was a contemporary of Elijah).

While the 400 prophets of Baal continued to predict elaborate stories of victory, Jehoshaphat insisted that Micaiah be brought in and consulted. So Ahab sent his most talented aide to summon Micaiah. As the messenger summoned Micaiah, he tried to convince him to go along with the majority: **"Look, as one man the other prophets are predicting success for the king. Let your word agree with theirs, and speak favorably." But Micaiah said, "As surely as the LORD lives, I can tell him only what my God says." So when Micaiah arrived, the king asked him, "Micaiah, shall we go to war against Ramoth Gilead, or shall I refrain?"**

Micaiah answered with great mocking sarcasm, **"Attack and be victorious, for they will be given into your hand."** Embarrassed, king Ahab lashed back, **"How many times must I make you swear to tell me nothing but the truth in the name of the LORD?"** This was obviously for show in front of Jehoshaphat. For Ahab had Micaiah put in prison for telling the truth in the name of the LORD. Ahab wanted the truth only if it agreed with his plan.

So Micaiah said, **"Then hear the word of the LORD, I saw the LORD sitting on His throne with all the host of heaven standing on His right and on His left. And He said, 'Who will go and entice**

Ahab into attacking Ramoth Gilead and going to his death there?'...One angel said, 'I will entice Ahab by putting a lying spirit in the mouths of all his prophets.' 'You will succeed in enticing him,' said the LORD. 'Go and do it.'

"So now the LORD has put a lying spirit in the mouths of these prophets of yours. The LORD has decreed disaster for you."

This prophecy infuriated Ahab. The chief of the false prophets slapped Michaiah across the face and mocked him by asking, "Which way did the spirit from the LORD go when he went from me to speak to you?" Micaiah prophesied to him and said, "You will find out on that day you try to hide in a secret room."

At this point Micaiah put himself and his prophetic gift to the test that Moses had commanded. **"Micaiah declared to King Ahab, 'If you ever return safely, the LORD has not spoken through me.' Then he challenged the people, 'Mark my words, all you people!'"**

Ahab even disguised himself as a common soldier, knowing the enemy would concentrate on killing the king with his elite soldiers. He took the added precaution of tricking king Jehoshaphat to wear the royal robes into battle. Even though the enemy charged straight for Jehoshapat, the LORD graciously saved him. But one of the enemy soldiers, just on a whim, fired a random arrow into the battle. The arrow fatally struck king Ahab in a tiny unprotected area where the armor joined together. Even though king Ahab tried to beat the odds, Micaiah's prediction was precisely fulfilled before sunset.

Micaiah was released from prison and received as

a true prophet. This is why his writings were put into the Bible and preserved, in spite of the fact that he and his prophecies were hated.

INVINCIBLE BABYLON FALLS IN A DAY

The first part of Daniel's remarkable prophecies involved the destruction and replacement of the great Babylonian Empire by the Media-Persians in his lifetime. Daniel first got this prophecy in his chapter two, which was at least 60 years before it happened.

At that time, Babylon was the most formidable power of history. They ruled the known world. The city of Babylon was considered impregnable. It had walls so thick that five chariots abreast could race around the top of this 150-foot-high fortress wall. The Euphrates River flowed through it, so water was plentiful. They grew food within the city so that it could withstand a long siege. There were great sharp iron bars that extended into the river to prevent soldiers from swimming into the city.

Daniel was called into a drunken feast celebrating Babylon's invincibility on the very day the Persians finished damming up and diverting the Euphrates River. Unknown to the overconfident Babylonians, the water began to recede slowly until nightfall. Then the Medes and Persians totally diverted the river and the water level fell rapidly under the cover of darkness. Since no one thought such a thing possible, no sentry observed the gathering catastrophe. The Medes and Persians swarmed under the wall through the dried-up river bed at about 3 am. Babylon fell the very day that Daniel interpreted **"the hand writing on the wall"**, which declared that the Acting Temporary King would die that day before sundown, and the empire would be taken over by the Medes and Persians. The odds seemed impossible for such a thing to happen. But God's Word was fulfilled to the letter. It usually does take a miracle for God's prophecies to be fulfilled—but no sweat, God is in the miracle business.

MIGHTY PERSIA TO FALL TO A BRASH YOUNG GREEK KING

More than two hundred years before Alexander the Great was born, and while the first world Empire, Babylon, was at the zenith of its power, Daniel predicted the Medes and Persians would form an alliance and conquer Babylon. Then the Greeks, whose five tribes had warred with each other for more than a century, would be united through an extraordinary king who would lead them to a victory over mighty Persia, which everyone thought would be impossible. The first, second and third world empires are predicted by name in Daniel chapter eight.

The sequences of history here are important. It shows clearly how amazingly the Hebrew prophets' predictions were literally fulfilled.

At the time of this vision, Babylon was the undisputed military power on earth. The Medes and the Persians had not yet formed an alliance and were no match for mighty Babylon. Yet at this very time, Daniel not only predicted the future Media-Persian Alliance's spectacular triumph. He also predicted that the Medes—who were strongest at first—would be taken over by the Persians later. He predicted that after Persia had become a wealthy and mighty world empire, they would be suddenly destroyed by the Greeks.

To understand how seemingly impossible this prediction about the Greeks was, you must look at their
immediate history and their condition at this time. The
Greeks were extremely advanced in knowledge, technology and culture. They were a brave people. But
they showed no promise of ever launching a military
campaign against a world power, much less a success-
ful one. The five tribes of Greeks were too busy fighting each other. They even spoke different dialects.

But then around the middle of the fourth century
BC, a mighty warrior king named Philip, who was from
the rugged tribal state of Macedonia, had a son he
named Alexander.

Alexander was educated personally by the great
Greek philosopher Aristotle. Alexander was a child
prodigy and genius, and the brilliant Aristotle took him
to his full potential. On the spiritual side, Alexander's
devoutly occultic mother taught him to believe as a
child that he was more than a mere man. She planted
the idea in him that he was destined for greatness, glory
and divinity. She knew that her husband Philip did not
like her and that her own survival was linked to the
success of her son. This vision of personal greatness
became the driving force of his life.

Even in Alexander's early teens, he would sneak
away from Aristotle and study his father's army as they
practiced various battle tactic and formations. During
those times he began to develop battle tactics and strategy that he knew would be better than his father's. At
eighteen years old he was already very restless to take
over from his aging father, who suffered from multiple
battle wounds, one of which was a crippled leg. But
Alexander's ambition and certainty that he was destined for greatness annoyed his father.

Then suddenly fate struck. The knife of a half-crazed assassin killed Philip on the steps of the Temple of Zeus and made Alexander an instant king. No one knew at the time that this assassin had just thrust onto the stage of history an eighteen-year-old boy who would forever alter its course. Though Alexander leaped to his father's aid and killed the assassin himself, a few believed that he had engineered the whole incident.

Legend has it that Alexander entered the Temple of Zeus right after his father's assassination. He took an oath and vowed he would bring more glory to Zeus and the gods of Greece than anyone in all history. He then made a strange request—he said, "I do not ask for a long life, but a short one. My only request is that it will be filled with victory in battle, wisdom with the conquered, and my name covered with immortal glory." Whether this actually happened or not, no one really knows. But it's certainly like something this larger-than-life personality would do. No one in human history so naturally fits the title of "The Great."

History shows that this ingenious young king invented a revolutionary new battle formation called the "phalanx." He also devised radical new tactics. His ability to quickly grasp a changing battle situation and instantly improvise a brilliant solution also kept the enemy generals off balance.

But most of all, it was Alexander's almost superhuman courage and bravery—and his daring, almost reckless audacity—that inspired his men to fight above their ability. He never ordered his men to go into battle. He always ordered, "Follow me." Alexander literally believed he could not be killed until his destiny was accomplished. He was at the forefront of virtually every battle. During his fighting career, thousands of arrows, lances, knives and swords were aimed at him, yet he was not killed in battle.

Why not? Because he was under the providence of the almighty God of the Bible. God's prophet Daniel had predicted that Alexander wouldn't die in battle. Though Daniel predicted he would die prematurely at a young age, he also predicted that this Greek king would conquer most of the known world before he died.

Upon assuming command of his father's army, he immediately began to train them in his new tactics. He prepared them quickly to launch a campaign to defeat and take over the other four tribes of Greece. In a shockingly quick time, Alexander did what no other Greek had been able to do. He not only conquered all of the other tribes, but convinced them to unite together into one nation. He was able to inspire them to see the potential of such a union.

Since they spoke in five dialects, Alexander, knowing that exact communication was essential in battle, fused together the best of the dialects and made one common language. This he did himself. His natural genius—plus the teaching of Aristotle, who above all was a brilliant linguist—enabled him to create a precise language for communicating exact thought. This dialect was named Koine Greek (Κοινη), which means "common Greek." Alexander commanded all the tribes to learn "the common language."

In less than two years as king, Alexander had Greece united and ready for conquest. Psychologically, the army was not ready to accept his lofty idea of conquering mighty Persia. So he took a popular cause and mobilized them for that. Alexander led his army across the Hellespont of the Aegean Sea, supposedly for a limited rescue operation of the oppressed Greeks living under Persian rule in what is now Turkey's western coastal regions. One of the first cities he "liberated" was ancient Troy. With lightning-like attacks, Alexander destroyed the Persian frontier military forces one after another. At this point, he had two secret purposes in mind. First, to give his men the confidence that comes with victory. Second, Alexander knew that he was provoking the proud King Darius to bring out his whole army. And he had positioned his force in such a way as to allow no easy escape. They would have to fight.

He was absolutely confident his army would win. To us looking back in history, it was a reckless all-or-nothing-at-all gamble. To Alexander, there was no risk. He was certain they would win—it was his destiny. His bravery and confidence became contagious.

Darius took the bait and with fatal overconfidence brought out his whole army with no real plan of attack, nor any attention to the strengths and weaknesses of the Greek army. The haughty Persians were sure this would be mostly a training exercise for them. They intended to teach the Greeks such a lesson that they would never dare to set foot in Persia again.

Alexander, on the other hand, knew the strengths and weaknesses of the Persians and had carefully planned to exploit them. He analyzed the approaching army and devised a plan that would quickly demoralize them and minimize their great numerical advantage. He picked out the battle flag of Persia's most elite battalion. He stalked them until just the right conditions of terrain partially isolated them. Moving with the speed and stealth of a leopard, he led his army in a daring attack against them. The Greeks destroyed them so quickly with their new phalanx maneuver that the rest of the Persian army was stunned. None of the Persian soldiers had ever seen anything like this. They were traumatized and never really regained their confidence and composure. In other words, Alexander had psyched them out!

Keeping the initiative, Alexander decoyed them to follow. He carefully picked the time and place for each attack. Sensing when the situation was right, he moved in for the decisive battle at Isis and Arbela. There the Greeks utterly decimated the remaining Persian army. The survivors panicked and fled in total disarray, leaving King Darius alone and unprotected. Two Persian deserters assassinated the defenseless Darius, thinking it would win them favor with Alexander. To their dismay, Alexander took pity on Darius and his dishonorable end. He was angry at the two deserters for their treachery and cowardice. He told them, "Only a king can execute a king." He drew his sword and killed them.

Almost before his army had fully grasped what was really happening, they had completely defeated the vaunted Persian army. Alexander realized that the kingdom of Persia was as helpless as their lifeless king. He savored the moment as he looked over his deliriously happy army. He had led them to do the impossible—they had conquered the leading power in the world.

The news of the incredible victory was quickly relayed to Athens. The Greek nation was stunned at the news. Their daring young king not only had liberated "the oppressed Greeks," but had conquered the seemingly invincible Persian empire, with all of its riches.

And once again, in an extraordinary way, Alexander had unknowingly fulfilled another part of

Daniel's 200 year old prophecy about his sudden conquest and takeover of Persia, the second world empire. The year was 331 BC.

From this time onward, Alexander's soldiers would follow him anywhere. They conquered everything in their path including the strategic land bridge that connected the three continents of Asia, Africa and Europe. This land bridge extended from Egypt northward to The Bosporus Straits at Byzantium, which is modern Istanbul. Then they fought eastward into India and the gateway to China.

MORE AMAZING PROVIDENCE AT WORK IN HISTORY

The Persian empire fell at Alexander's feet. Instead of making them slaves and treating them cruelly, he required them only to embrace the Greek culture and language. For the most part, he made friends of them. This too was a fulfillment of God's providential use of him. Unwittingly, Alexander was being used to accomplish God's purpose by making Koine Greek the lingua franca of the known world.

Even Rome would not be able to change the universal language. When the remains of the Greek empire were taken over by the Romans, everyone continued to use Greek as the language of business, trade and international communication.

So when Jesus the Messiah came and purchased a pardon for the sin of all mankind by his death under our judgment, the infinitely valuable message about it was entrusted to none other than Alexander's creation—Koine Greek. The original manuscript of the New Testament was written in this Common Greek and could be rapidly spread among the Gentiles. Why?

Because in the providential working of God, Alexander had made it possible for them to understand.

AN IMPORTANT FOOTNOTE IN HISTORY

Another amazing footnote of history which is enormously important: when later Alexander began his conquest southward toward Egypt, he conquered most of Israel and besieged Jerusalem. The High Priest requested an audience, and showed Alexander that his whole life and career had been foreknown and predicted by Israel's God more than two hundred years before. He taught Alexander from the second, seventh and eighth chapters of Daniel. It is said that Alexander fell down and declared Yaweh, the LORD of Israel, the God of gods. Also he spared Jerusalem and took with him many of the royal family of Judah and made them royal administrators of his conquered kingdoms. Jews were spread throughout the empire. Because of this, it later became necessary for the Hellenized Jews to have a Greek translation of their Hebrew Bible. The translation, known as the Septuagint (or LXX) for the Seventy translators, was completed in 165 BC in a city founded by and named for Alexander—Alexandria, Egypt. Thus, long before His birth, there were now available for the Gentile world the prophecies of the Messiah's coming as a humble servant who would provide a way to God for all peoples.

THE AMAZING EIGHTH CHAPTER OF DANIEL

The prophecy in Daniel chapter 8 clearly describes Alexander's career and destiny. It even predicts

Alexander's premature death at the height of his career. A very unusual twist in normal tradition was also predicted. Daniel 8 (verses 20 through 22) predicts that after Alexander's premature death his empire would be divided into four spheres of power.

Normally, the king would have given the empire to his son, who was with him at his death. But instead, when on his death bed he was asked, "To whom do you will your kingdom?" he replied, "Give it to the strong." And the strong quickly took it over. The four senior generals of his army took it over and divided it into four kingdoms. They were generals Lysimachus, Cassander, Ptolemy and Seleucus.

Lysimachus took Macedonia and Greece as far south as Athens. Cassander took Asia Minor. Seleucus took Syria and the regions eastward up to old Persia. Ptolemy took Egypt and parts of North Africa.

Lysimachus then murdered Alexander's son and his widow, Roxanne. So no blood heir survived to ever contest the new order of the Empire that had been established.

Thus Daniel's prophecy about Alexander and Greece, the third Gentile World Empire, was fulfilled in all its parts, in spite of all the odds against its happening.

ROME'S RISE TO WORLD DOMINANCE PREDICTED

Daniel in the same prophecy about the four successive world-conquering empires, which is found in Daniel chapters 2, 7 and 8, predicted that the remains of the Greek Empire would be taken over by the mightiest world power of them all—Rome. He predicted that the fourth empire, which is Rome, would not be destroyed then, but would disintegrate from within and go into a mystery form until the time just before the King-Messiah's Second Coming, after which He would destroy it and replace it with His own.

A critical prophecy about a Roman Empire phase two in the last days is the following: **"Thus he said: 'The fourth beast will be a fourth kingdom on the earth, which will be different from all the other kingdoms, and it will devour the whole earth and tread it down and crush it. As for the ten horns, OUT OF this kingdom ten kings will arise; and ANOTHER [the Antichrist] will arise after them, and he will be different from the previous ones and will subdue three kings [of the ten]...'"** (Daniel 7:23-24 NASB).

This prophecy reveals that there would be only four kingdoms that would have world authority. *Out of* the ruins of the old Roman culture and people will arise a second phase of the fourth kingdom in the form of a ten nation confederacy. After the ten nations unite and rise to power, a uniquely different kind of power and leader will arise. He will take over the ten and subdue three leaders in the process. Under the Roman Antichrist's leadership, the fourth kingdom will reach its greatest world dominion, actually bringing all the nations of the world under its control for three and a half years. This form of Gentile power will confront the Messiah Himself. It will be destroyed by the Messiah and be replaced by His kingdom for the rest of history.

SOMETHING TO CONSIDER

Can we believe this is really going to happen? Consider this—Daniel established himself as a true prophet within his own generation. He predicted years before it occurred that Babylon would be conquered by the Medes and Persians. Against all odds, it happened. He even predicted that the Persians would dominate the Medes after the kingdom was established. So by the test of Moses he was recognized as a true prophet and his writings were included in the Hebrew Bible.

These illustrations of literally fulfilled prophecy, confirmed by history, are only a few of hundreds of examples contained in the Bible. They establish the unique qualifications of a true Biblical prophet.

CAN WE BELIEVE THE EXTRAORDINARY PREDICTIONS ABOUT OUR IMMEDIATE FUTURE?

I have been intrigued and amazed by all kinds of prophets, both in past history and in our day. Nostradamus, Mayan Calendar interpreters, Hopi Indian prophecies, Jean Dixon, New Age prophets, channelers, palm readers, astrologers, tarot cards, etc. All are interesting, but none come close to the prophets of the Bible. They either had a 100% record of accuracy or at best their writings were burned and they were cast out as a false prophet, or at the worst, they were stoned to death for speaking lies in the name of the LORD. Because of this, we can trust the prophecies of the true prophets about the future to be literally fulfilled, no matter what the odds or degree of difficulty. Please consider this as we explore some extraordinary events that were predicted at least two thousand years ago or earlier, but now are beginning to be fulfilled before our eyes.

THE CHARGE OF THE FOUR HORSEMEN

CHAPTER FOUR

"The earth is polluted by its people; they have disobeyed the laws, violated the statutes and broken the everlasting covenant. Therefore a curse devours the earth , and those who live in it are held guilty. Therefore, the inhabitants of the earth are burned, and very FEW MEN ARE LEFT."
—Isaiah the Prophet: 24:5, 6. (750 BC)

CONFESSIONS OF A TIME TRAVELER

Imagine, if you can, a day in the not-too-distant future when the planet will be turned into a living hell. The source of the judgment will be God Himself, although He will use the fallen nature of man and the natural systems of the earth as the vehicles of a near-total destruction of the planet.

At least 2-billion-plus people will be killed in a relatively short period—perhaps only a few months. These four great apocalyptic catastrophes are described by the coded symbols of four dreadful

Horsemen who are presented in the first eight verses of The Apocalypse, chapter 6.

The Apostle John didn't have to imagine the horrors he described. He witnessed them firsthand—with his own eyes and ears. He recorded exactly what he saw and heard. The only problem is that he witnessed 21st century events with first century experiences. Like a time traveler, he was physically transported 2000 years into the future and was commanded to write an accurate eyewitness account. We only imagine such a possibility in fiction, but a number of Biblical prophets describe being transported centuries into the future to witness firsthand a war of such magnitude that their ancient experiences could barely supply phenomena from their century to symbolize the marvels of technology and science they witnessed in what we see as the beginning of the 21st century.

Think of John not as a poet, nor a fictional novelist, as many so-called "biblical scholars" have through the years. The Apocalypse is not an allegory. It is not a collection of mysterious, unintelligible symbolism. It is not fiction. It is not arcane mumbo-jumbo. It is a living, breathing, prophetic and historical account of events yet to take place. It was written to be understood by the generation that was near the fulfillment of the astounding things predicted to immediately precede the Coming of Jesus the Messiah. I believe we are that generation.

IS THERE EVIDENCE OF AN IMMINENT APOCALYPSE?

"You're losing me, Hal," you might say at this point. "History that has yet to take place? Is there such a thing?" You bet there is!

First, I believe this is the only generation for which most of the prophecies of the Apocalypse apply. This is the only generation in history that has witnessed the coming together of the whole predicted scenario to precede the Messiah's Second Coming.

The following is a list of some of the fulfillments of this predicted scenario:

- the return of the Jews to the land of Israel and the formation of a state in spite of centuries of persecution wherever they fled
- the Israeli recapture of old Jerusalem
- the rise of Russia as a dangerous rogue military power with an awesome arsenal of lethal weapons inherited from the USSR
- the rise of Islamic nations as a major power with their relentless pursuit of Jerusalem and Israel's destruction
- the entrance of China as a world class power and the rise of Asia as the most populated and technically skilled area in the world
- the uniting of European nations into a single awesome power after centuries of fighting with each other
- the simultaneous increase in frequency and magnitude of war, earthquakes, plagues, famines, super storms, global warming and global weather pattern changes.

Remember what I said earlier in this book. First and foremost, John was a prophet claiming to speak directly from and for God. This put him in that special category that required him to pass Moses' test of a true prophet (Deuteronomy 18:15-18). His very life, therefore, depended on 100 percent accuracy in all of his predictions.

BACK TO THE FUTURE

Though the Apostle John had the most unique experience of being catapulted into the distant future, he was not the only one. As I said above, a few Old Testament prophets clearly experienced the same sort of extraordinary "time travel" to the era of the seven-year-tribulation period—especially to witness the most devastating and catastrophic war of all times.

John was, however, catapulted by God from one time period to another so that his extensive "visions" would have the authority of an eyewitness. The prophet then unknowingly encoded a warning for the generation in which these things would happen with conviction, accuracy and authority.

In view of everything I've learned, I firmly believe this is that generation to which John was writing. Let's take our view from the beginning of the 21st century and interpret what he has to say about events that will soon consume our world—a seven-year period of the greatest Tribulation this earth has ever seen or will ever see.

What do I mean by "Tribulation"? We've all heard the term. We often associate tribulations with trials—tests of hardship and suffering. The dictionary defines tribulation as "great misery or distress, as from oppression." It means "deep sorrows due to affliction." But the Greek word θλιψις, as used in the New Testament, means much more. Its coded meaning is carefully developed to mean a special time of great distress and suffering that is unparalleled in all of human history. It will virtually destroy the earth. The first half is terrible, but the last three and a half years are beyond imagination.

The word "great" is added to "tribulation" to describe the last half of this period. Daniel the prophet says of this period, **"...There will be a time of distress such as has not happened from the beginning of nations until then..."** (Daniel 12:1 NIV). Jesus predicted similarly of this period, **"For then there will be a great tribulation such as has not been from the beginning of the world until then, and never under any circumstances shall be again. And if those days had not been cut short, no human being would be left alive"** (Matthew 24:21-22). Jeremiah also prophesied about this period, **"How awful that day will be! None will be like it. It will be the time of Jacob's trouble, but he will be saved out of it"** (Jeremiah 30:7). All of this immediately precedes the Second Advent of Jesus, the Messiah.

The beginning of those sorrows is described in Revelation 6:1-8, an account which reveals the enigmatic "four horsemen of the Apocalypse". They are the first four seals of the Book of the Apocalypse, which contain encrypted, coded messages meant to be understood fully for the first time by this generation of earthlings. Daniel's command to shut up, encode and seal the scroll of prophecy until the time of the end is fulfilled in this generation.

Until this point in the Apocalypse, John seems to be overwhelmed—perhaps in awe of what he has been shown. But now He sees the great scroll of God containing the decreed judgments of the world. The first wax seal which fastens it shut is broken. The document is unrolled to the next wax seal. Out of each unrolled section comes a new judgment with new terrors for the whole world. It is the unleashing of very specific horrors, each getting progressively worse on a geometric scale.

THE JUDGE WITH WOUNDED HANDS AND FEET

No wonder only Jesus could qualify to open the seals, according to chapter five of the Apocalypse. He is the divine person who condescended to take upon himself a true human nature so that He could qualify to die for the sins of, and in place of, all other humans. Thus He alone is qualified to judge those who rejected His offer of free pardon which He purchased with His own blood. He did all He could to save mankind from their own righteous judgment by bearing it in their place. But if an individual rejects the only solution for offending God's perfect justice, there is nothing more He can do.

Then John's whole demeanor seemed to change. As the first seal was broken, John himself must have been terrified by what he saw. His vision of Jesus changed from Savior to Judge, from Lamb to Lion.

I've said it before and I'll say it again, the sight of catastrophes of such magnitude as he describes must have brought terror and a sense of foreboding to John. I'm certain the hand that penned these verses must have been trembling.

But what is he describing? First of all, the command "come" in chapter six, verse 1 and subsequent verses should actually be translated "go." Why? Because the translation of the Greek word used here is determined by its context. In this context, a mighty Angel gives the command for each seal to be broken. He authorizes the rider of the white horse to begin his campaign of conquest on the earth. "**Go**," he says. The literal idea is, "**Charge forth and do the evil in your heart.**"

THE FIRST SEAL: The World Receives The Messiah It Sought

"Now I saw when the Lamb opened one of the seals; and I heard one of the four living creatures saying with a voice like thunder, 'Come and see.' And I looked, and behold, a white horse. And he who sat on it had a bow; and a crown was given to him, and he went out conquering and to conquer" (Revelation 6:1–2).

Who is the rider of this white horse? It's the one known as the Antichrist of Rome—the **future fuhrer**, as I called him in *The Late Great Planet Earth*. He will become supreme dictator over more people than any leader in all of history.

He will mesmerize people to worship him. All nations and peoples will happily bestow on him absolute authority over everything.

In the symbolism of the ancient world, a crowned king riding on a white horse stood for victory in conquest. When a military leader victoriously entered a newly conquered kingdom, invariably he would ride a white horse.

Notice this conqueror carries with him a warrior's bow. Why did John use the symbol of a **"bow"** instead of the usual code word for war—a **"sword"**? It could be that a sword was used for close-in hand-to-hand combat. But the **bow** was a long-range weapon that could hurl a missile a long way. This is a code for long range weapons like ICBMs. It also implies the Antichrist will use the threat of war rather than actual war to conquer. Altogether it symbolizes his control over the lethal weapons of war. On his head rests a **crown**, for he will seduce virtually all of the peoples of the earth. Eventually, as we'll see later, the whole world will claim him as their savior and benevolent dictator.

WHO IS THIS GUY?

This Antichrist will be a European. He will be a man of great magnetism and power—a messianic-type figure who will seem to have answers to all the world's problems. He will be extremely charismatic, attractive, even beguiling. He will dazzle the world with miracles produced by the power of Satan, who will possess him body and soul.

We know this because the Bible clearly tells us that the Roman Empire, which ruled over the world at the time of Christ, will be revived during this period of tribulation, perhaps even in response to aspects of the global crisis. To understand how we know this, you must first go back to the Old Testament—to Daniel 7, known by the scribes as the greatest chapter in the Hebrew scriptures. Jesus and His apostles referred to it many times during their ministry. But, still, much of it—like the Apocalypse—remained obscure until our times.

The real background of this person was received by Daniel in a dream. In this dream he saw four great beasts come out of the sea. The first beast was like a lion, but had eagle's wings. The second beast was like a bear; the third beast was like a leopard, but had four heads. The fourth animal was "dreadful and terrible" — it had iron teeth and 10 horns. What did all this mean? Well, fortunately for Daniel, an Angel explained that the great beasts represented **"four kingdoms**, which shall arise out of the earth."

WORLD EMPIRES
ALL PREDICTED

The first kingdom was **Babylon**, which became a world empire in 606 B.C. when it conquered Egypt. Nebuchadnezzar took over the empire from his father and turned it into a world kingdom. The second kingdom world government was the **Media-Persian Empire.** The Babylonians were conquered by the Medes and the Persians about 530 B.C. About two hundred years later, the **Greeks** became the third empire when Alexander the Great conquered the mighty Persians.

Daniel deciphers his own prophetic code in chapter eight. An Angel explains to him, **"The ram which you saw with two horns represents the kings of Media and Persia"** (Daniel 8:20). This interprets the coded symbols of the first part of chapter 8, in which the ram conquers Babylon and all powers around its Empire. The **two horns** represent **Media and Persia**. The fact that the most powerful horn came up last accurately describes what later happened. The **Medes** were the most powerful when **Babylon** was conquered. But then **Persia** became the most powerful and took over permanently.

"And the shaggy goat represents the kingdom of Greece, and the large horn that is between his eyes is the first king [Alexander the Great]" (Daniel 8:21). How accurately this predicts history two-hundred-plus years before it happened! Alexander became King at a very young age. As we have seen, his military genius enabled him to conquer the five tribes of Greece and to unite them into one force and nation. He also created a common form of the Greek language from the five different dialects so that he could give an order and it would not be misunderstood; this later became the Greek in which the New Testament was written. It is the most accurate language in the world if the laws of grammar and syntax are followed. No wonder it powerfully expresses God's will.

"And the broken horn and the four horns that arose in its place represent four kingdoms which will arise from his nation, although not with his power" (Daniel 8:22). As stated earlier, when Alexander prematurely died at the age of 33 he was asked as a formality, "To whom do you will your empire?" Alexander's son was at his bedside, and all expected Alexander to name his son as his successor. But he shocked all when he declared, "Give it to the strong." And the strong took it. Alexander's four leading generals divided up the empire into four parts and took over. They were Ptolemy, Seleucus, Lysimachus and Cassandar. This was such a phenomenal fulfillment of prophecy that unbelieving scholars of the 19th and 20th centuries have tried to late date Daniel so that the prophecy would be written after the fact and thus not so miraculous. But the integrity of Daniel's early date has been ably defended.

But around 68 B.C., the fourth and greatest kingdom seized world power from the remains of Alexander's weakened and divided kingdom. Rome, you will notice, was not given the name of any animal in Daniel's dream, but it was described as fierce. In phase one, this kingdom gained world authority, then it crumbled and fell. But it will rise again, the scriptures promise.

In this second phase of the fourth kingdom, Rome will take the form of a 10-nation confederacy. And the man heading up this revived Roman Empire will be the one known as the Antichrist—the rider of the white horse.

Notice that this character—this person himself—is presented as the first of the great judgments of God upon a world that has rejected Him and His Son. The world will turn to this phony—this counterfeit messiah. But, instead of a savior, he will turn out to be the world's greatest curse. Jesus warned about this clever imposter, **"I have come in My Father's name, and you do not receive me. If another shall come in his own name, you will receive him"** (John 5:43).

THE SECOND SEAL:
War Shatters Pseudo-Peace

"When He opened the second seal, I heard the second living creature saying, 'Come and see.' And another horse, fiery red, went out. And it was granted to the one who sat on it to take peace from the earth, and that people should kill one another; and there was given to him a great sword" (The Apocalypse 6:3-4).

What is this **"sword"**? It is a Biblical code phrase often used as a symbol of the lethal weapons of war. The addition of the word **"great"** expands the idea to stress an enormous arsenal of deadly weapons. When John was launched to the future, he witnessed a terrifying, global holocaust fought with weapons of enormous destructive power. He witnessed these weapons quickly cause the annihilation of hundreds of millions of people. He witnessed the virtual obliteration of the earth's life-sustaining ecological systems. Such phenomena must have been almost beyond his first-century comprehension. I believe this experience must have so shocked John's mind that it would have destroyed his sanity apart from the presence of the Spirit of God sustaining him.

So the Rider of the Red Horse releases for use this tremendous arsenal of mass destruction, and the rebellious nature of man quickly uses them. I believe that up until this moment, God graciously restrained the all-out use of these scientific marvels of death and destruction. The Apostle Paul warned of the last-days removal of God's protective restraining influence through the Holy Spirit's special residence in the world in the mystical true Church. But at this point of the well-defined scenario of predicted future events, all living true believers from within the various denominations of the visible Church will have been instantly and mysteriously removed. And the special age of the Holy Spirit's residence in the world in the true believers will have ended with the same event. This event, commonly called the Rapture, reverses Pentecost, and the Holy Spirit returns basically to His Old Testament ministry (2 Thessalonians 2:1-13).

KEY POINTS OF FUTURE HISTORY

At first, remember, this Roman Antichrist brings a pseudo-peace to the world during his first three-and-one-half years of consolidating total world authority. Everyone will be singing his praises as the greatest leader in the history of the world. He is praised not only for his superhuman intelligence, but also for his aura of deep spirituality and vision for bringing all mankind to a quantum leap in consciousness that is promised to bring a new, higher order of life.

But at the **mid-point** of the seven-year tribulation, the second seal is opened. Jesus gave the great historical sign to indicate that the last half of the seven-year Tribulation period was about to begin: **"Therefore when you see the Abomination that causes Desolation which was spoken of through Daniel the prophet, standing in the holy place** [of the rebuilt Temple] **(let the reader understand), then let those who are in Judea flee to the mountains, let him who is on the housetop not go down to get the things out of his house; and let him who is in the field not turn back to get his cloak . . . For then there will be a great tribulation, such as has not occurred since the beginning of the world until now, nor ever shall again. And unless those days had been cut short, no life would have been saved . . ."** (Matthew 24:15-18, 21-22 NASB).

The timing of this corresponds to Daniel's prediction (Daniel 11:31, 12:11) of this final allotment of seven years to Israel: **"And he** [the Antichrist from Rome] **will make a covenant of protection with the many** [Israelites] **for one week** [a sabbath of seven years], **but in the middle of the week** [3 1/2 years] **he will put a stop to sacrifice and grain offering; and on the wing of Abominations will come one who makes desolate, even until a decreed complete destruction is poured out on the One who makes desolate."**

UNDERSTAND "THE ABOMINATION THAT CAUSES DESOLATION"

This passage, though complicated, gives the precise timing of these momentous events. **"The Abomination"** takes place when the Roman Antichrist enters the Holiest Place of the soon-to-be-rebuilt Jerusalem Temple, takes his seat on the Ark of the Covenant, and proclaims himself to be God (see 2 Thessalonians 2:3-4). This ultimate act of human arrogance triggers the **war to end all wars.** Ezekiel's long-predicted invasion sweeps into Israel with the pent-up-fury of four thousand years of hatred that started with Ishmael and was later enshrined by his descendants in the Muslim religion.

Israel will be duped into a false sense of security, foolishly trusting in the treaty made with the Roman Antichrist that guarantees their protection and safety. So just as Ezekiel predicted long ago, they will be unprepared for this sudden flood of invading Russian and Muslim troops.

This shatters the world's illusion of peace. I believe this **rider of the red horse** launches the great power from the extreme north of Israel, as predicted in Ezekiel 38 and 39 and Daniel 11:40–45. The forefathers of this mighty invading confederacy are listed by Ezekiel and have been easily identified today. Thus begins the war of Armageddon, which escalates to involve the whole world.

Ezekiel traces the course of this terrible war: **"Then you will come from your place out of the extreme north, you and many peoples with you, all of them riding horses, a great company and a**

mighty army. You will come up against My people Israel like a cloud, to cover the land. It will be in the latter days that I will bring you against My land, so that the nations may know Me, when I am hallowed in you, O Gog, before their eyes" (Ezekiel 38: 15–16).

THREE IMPERATIVE CLUES FROM EZEKIEL'S PROPHECY

First remember the **time clue**. This invasion could happen only after the rebirth of the State of Israel in the last days—specifically at a time when the land has been turned into an unprecedented desolation, and when the Israelites, who have been scattered for centuries among all the nations of the world, are miraculously returned to re-establish the State of Israel.

Second, **the geographical clue**. The only nation to the extreme north of Israel, from which all prophecies are reckoned, is the Republic of Russia.

Third, **the ethnic-genealogy clue**. The modern ethnic Russian is descended from the Scythians, who are descended from the ancient tribe of Magog.

RUSSIA'S FATAL HOOKED HARNESS

Russia's chief partner in that invasion is Persia, or modern-day Iran (Ezekiel 38:5). Did you know that intelligence experts are now calling the Moscow-Tehran alliance one of the most important fixtures of the Post-Cold War era? It's true. My friend Joseph de Courcy, editor of *Intelligence Digest*, points out that Iran is capable of spreading the Islamic revolution throughout Central Asia, the Transcaucasus and into the Muslim regions of Russia itself. No one is more aware of this threat than the leaders of Russia. They were forced to sign a pact with Iran out of fear of this potentially disastrous development. The pact guarantees Iran use of their top nuclear and missile scientists, access to every weapon in their arsenal and a commitment to fight alongside Iran against the West in the event of any future armed interference against them.

But Iran has only one priority on its foreign policy agenda—the destruction of the State of Israel. Ezekiel talks about a day, in the not-too-distant future, in which Russia will be inexorably drawn into a conflict in the Middle East.

Ezekiel's prophecy indicates that this invasion will occur almost against Russia's own will. Ezekiel's illustration of "a hook in the jaw of the Russian leader" refers to a donkey bridle made with cruel hooks on both sides that dug into a stubborn donkey's jaw when he refused to follow his master. Every day it becomes more clear just what that "hook in Russia's jaw" will be—the alliance Russia made with the growing Islamic powers of the Middle East, led by the fanatical Islamic Fundamentalists of Iran.

Both Ezekiel and Revelation make it clear that it is God who places that hook in Russia's jaw. Yet, Russia has historically been an expansionist power itself—one with a particular long-term interest in the lands that lie directly to its south. Even in "democratic" Russia, a government agency has been actively studying the possibility of nuclear weapons cooperation with Iran, Libya, Iraq and Algeria—all named as part of the Magog coalition that invades Israel in Ezekiel 38. Russia is even working a contingency plan for a full-scale military alliance with Tehran.

NEVER FORGET THE ARSENAL CONTROLLED BY RUSSIA

Keep in mind, Russia still commands the largest arsenal of nuclear arms and other weapons of mass destruction in history, inherited from the old USSR. The latest reliable estimates show that Russia has 109 strategic bombers equipped with 1,374 nuclear warheads, at least 887 intercontinental ballistic missiles with 4,833 nuclear warheads, and at least 456 sea-launched missiles with 2,320 nuclear warheads. Additionally, Russia still maintains a vast arsenal of biological and chemical arms and there are reports of secret high-tech superweapons in its stockpile. The agreement with the West to destroy their nuclear forces is a pitiful joke. All the Russians have done is to destroy their obsolete missiles with some of their silos. Now they have mobile ICBMs (the SS-25 and SS-26) that are far deadlier, and far more accurate and reliable.

But it is Russia's direct alliance with Iran that is one of the most prophetically significant developments in the world today.

"Iran's ultimate goal is to be the undisputed leader of the Islamic world—and the way it hopes to achieve this is by delivering Jerusalem to Islam," explains de Courcy. "With so much of the [current] Arab world firmly in the western camp—particularly the oil-rich states of the Arabian peninsula—and with Israel's military machine maintaining its regional dominance through American aid, the only way in which Iran can achieve its aim is through a strategic alliance with Moscow." It is immensely significant to see how some of the best of the secular intelligence community are coming to the same conclusions as those of Bible prophecy experts.

This imminent war, led by the Rider on the Red Horse, escalates until it involves all the major powers of the world. It begins the greatest conflict in history, centered around the plains of Armageddon. No, this is not a battle, as it is often called. Armageddon is an all-out war, an expanding holocaust of epic proportions, which includes many battles. But the **"War of Armageddon"** doesn't seem to be confined only to the valley underneath the ancient mountain fortress of Meggido, which is the root of its name. The vortex of the war seems to continue there, but it escalates to wreak destruction worldwide.

THE THIRD SEAL: Famine And Plague

"When He opened the third seal, I heard the third living creature say, 'Come and see.' And I looked, and behold, a black horse, and he who sat on it had a pair of scales in his hand. And I heard a voice in the midst of the four living creatures saying, 'A quart of wheat for a denarius, and three quarts of barley for a denarius; and do not harm the oil and the wine'" (Revelation 6:5-6).

Once global war breaks out—a war identified with the use of advanced weapons of mass destruction—there are bound to be some major disruptions and dislocations in the world economic system. The way food, fuel, medicine and other life-supporting commodities are distributed will certainly be turned into chaos.

One saying I have noted as a student of history: the hungrier people get, the itchier become their trigger fingers. This is a code-symbol used in the Bible to indicate great scarcity of food. The pair of scales referred to in the opening of the third seal indicates the world's population is facing severe food shortages. Food is being weighed out as carefully as gold.

How bad will it get? Look at the mathematics here. A day's ration of wheat will cost a denarius—the Biblical equivalent of a day's pay. In other words, during the Tribulation, the average man will have to pay out his entire day's salary just to purchase meager food rations for his family. And what's this about oil and wine? These, of course, were the symbols of luxury foods in John's day. The horseman instructs the average person not to even hope for these items. Why? Perhaps they will be used to tempt people. After all, only the rich will be able to function in a normal way economically during this period. In order to retain wealth, at this point, it will be necessary to sell out to the Antichrist. Imagine how tempting the finer luxuries in life—good cuisine, luxurious homes, reliable means of transportation—will look when most of the world is literally starving.

GROWING SIGNS
OF GLOBAL FOOD SHORTAGE

The truth is, you know, that the world is headed for a major food crisis even without the impact of a major global conflagration. With the third world's population expected to grow by 2 billion people in the next few years, developing countries will need at least 75 percent more food than they are currently producing. Yet, food production globally is growing at its slowest rate in four decades and is on the decline in 90 countries. Grain stocks, in fact, are at their lowest levels in 35 years. By the year 2030, China alone will require all of the world's current exports of grain.

As usual, one of the biggest contributing factors to man's problems is his inability or unwillingness to heed the time-proven Biblical principles—in this case, with regard to periodic rotation of crops to allow the soil to rest and replenish itself. We're just too smart to learn anything from the tried-and-true concepts of the Old Testament. But just take the crisis of soil erosion and depletion we are experiencing today. Have you ever had a beautiful but tasteless tomato? Did you know that the ancient Israelites were commanded to give the soil a rest every seven years? That rest allowed the land to recover its nutrients. Modern industrialized farming makes no such allowances. Once soil fertility is depleted, crops will not produce without increasing levels of chemical fertilizers. And what's wrong with that?

There is grave doubt about how much chemical fertilizer some soils can take without deterioration. At some point, we know, heavy fertilization becomes counterproductive. Some experts believe we are reaching that point in some industrialized countries—the very nations that serve as the breadbasket to the world. Can anyone spare a denarius?

Modern agricultural techniques are also putting a severe strain on the world's water resources. Water tables are being depleted at alarming rates—even in the United States. Irrigation is also leaving millions upon millions of acres of productive farmland desolate from salinization and erosion. In the past, these kinds of problems have destroyed entire civilizations. Water scarcity is a spreading global problem and, some say, will be the central source of tension among nations that could lead to war.

GLOBAL WEATHER CHANGES AND THE LOSS OF FARM LAND

Another contributing problem is the striking change in global weather patterns observed by scientists during the last generation. The unpredictable—and sometimes deadly—weather of recent years has many climate researchers convinced global warming is a reality.

"After the mid-1970s, suddenly everything started looking really erratic," explains Nick Graham, a climate researcher at the Scripps Institute of Oceanography in La Jolla, California. "Everything changed here. We had dry falls. We had winters that were wetter. And it wasn't just here, it was climate change all over the world."

Imagine what a sustained worldwide drought—lasting several years—would mean to the planet in its current state. Or, what would an increase in world temperatures of a degree or two mean? Those prospects appear very possible—perhaps even likely—in the next few years.

BIRTH PANGS OF ARMAGEDDON

I do not pretend to predict the future the way the Apostle John or any other inspired prophet of the Bible did. But I do know that famine is going to be a reality for the world in this generation. Like other **"signs of the times"**, they will increase in frequency and intensity in the days ahead.

How can I be so sure? Because the Bible explicitly lays out the prophetic scenario we now see being fulfilled. When asked by His disciples how the world would know the general time of His return to earth, Jesus said, **"Take heed that no one deceives you.**

For many will come in My name, saying, 'I am the Messiah,' and will deceive many. And you will hear of wars and rumors of wars. See that you are not troubled; for all these things must come to pass, but the end is not yet. For ethnic group will rise against ethnic group, and kingdom against kingdom. And there will be famines, plagues, and great earthquakes in various places. All these things are merely the beginning of the birth pangs" (Matthew 24:4-8, literal translation from the Greek).

Does that sound at all like life here on planet earth in the latter part of the 20th century? The key to identifying this scenario of predictions as a genuine sign of the times is the code word "birth pangs." For just as a woman about to give birth experiences birth pangs in increasing frequency and intensity, so all these predicted catastrophes will increase in frequency and magnitude in concert with each other.

PLAGUES AND THE DECLINE OF ANTIBIOTICS

Notice also that Matthew mentions the coming of "pestilence or plague." You might expect diseases and plagues to run rampant in a world consumed by war and wracked by hunger and economic calamity. But the scope of the pandemics already gripping the world are beyond the ability of most of us to understand. Take AIDS, for instance. The number infected is already nearing the 100 million mark. This is triple what the World Health Organization had projected.

Scientists learned in the last couple of years that there are different strains of AIDS coexisting in people, blending genetic material from subtypes and spawning new hybrids of the deadly virus. This means that even if a vaccine is developed for one strain, it may not protect against the seven or eight others.

AIDS already is sweeping through Southeast Asia in the same way it cut a swath across Africa a decade ago. Within five years, the World Health Organization expects 4 million to be infected in Thailand alone. In Africa, an estimated 11 million already have the disease. AIDS is now the leading cause of death among Americans ages 25 to 44, according to the Centers for Disease Control. And that's just AIDS.

THE DRUG RESISTANT SUPER-STRAINS OF OLD DISEASES

"AIDS does not stand alone," explains Laurie Garrett in her book, *The Coming Plague*. "It may well be just the first of the modern, large-scale epidemics of infectious disease."

Difficult as it may be to believe, some of the others may actually be worse. As Richard Preston, author of *The Hot Zone*, says: "AIDS takes 10 years to kill its victim. The Ebola virus can take as little as 10 hours."

Preston's book and the Hollywood movie hit *Outbreak* helped persuade Americans of the increasing danger of killer viruses, including many thought only recently to be extinct or under control. Cholera, dengue, yellow fever, diphtheria, tuberculosis and other infections are increasing exponentially throughout the world. In an age of supersonic international travel, it's a wonder the outbreaks haven't been worse.

Flesh-eating bacteria, the Marburg virus, whooping cough, Cryptosporidium, toxic shock—the list goes on and on. The world has already entered a deadly new age of plagues. Compounding the problem is the fact that antibiotics, antivirals and other medicines are now failing to cure many of these diseases. The failure of modern medicine is contributing to a resurgence of Lyme disease, Legionnaires' disease, malaria, influenza and many other bacterial infections.

God has always dealt harshly with plagues, especially those linked with sin. In Romans 1:27, the Apostle Paul warned that homosexuals would pay a natural consequence for their sexual immorality—"the due penalty of their error." There is a physical price to pay for living this lifestyle, according to the Bible. But then this sort of straight talk is politically incorrect today.

But it's not just homosexual sin that bears such a price. The Bible also recounts a time when the Israelites were faced with a plague in the Plains of Moab after an orgy with prostitutes. Moses contained the diseases by killing every potential carrier on direct orders from God. Nevertheless, the Book of Numbers (25:1-9) says that 24,000 died from that plague.

What John is telling us in the Apocalypse is that the world is headed for a total ecosystem breakdown—complicated by terrible armed conflicts, political and ethnic struggles and, lastly, a spiritual war waged by powerful forces loosed for the first time in millennia. This brings us to the fourth seal.

THE FOURTH SEAL: Four Faces Of Death

"When He opened the fourth seal, I heard the voice of the fourth living creature saying, 'Come and see.' And I looked, and behold a pale

horse. And the name of him who sat on it was
Death, and Hades followed with him. And power
was given to them over a fourth of the earth, to
kill with sword, with hunger, with death, and by
the beasts of the earth" (Revelation 6:7–8).

"**Wild beasts of the earth?**" you may well be
thinking. "Are you kidding? Hal, what are we talking
about here? This all sounds like Greek to me." Well, let
me translate that phrase into something that will look
like Greek to you. Why? Because it is.

Και υπο των θηριων της γης. That's what the
above phrase looks like in Greek. When the preposition υπο is used with the genitive case, it means "by the
direct personal agency of"—in this case "the wild
beasts of the earth." This preposition can best be
understood by the contemporary English slang expression "up close and personal." That's the way these wild
beasts will kill. These beasts will really do some personal chewing—almost as if it were a frantic revenge
for mankind's pollution and destruction of their
domain.

What are these "wild beasts"? The term is used
both literally and figuratively in the New Testament.
The preposition (υπο) of personal agency tends to
push the meaning toward the figurative sense. The
same word is used in Titus 1:12 in the sense of "a person with a bestial nature." It is also used in the sense of
"wild, animal-like beings of a supernatural kind." So it
could be used in the figurative sense of demon-possessed leaders who, like the supreme leader of this
domain—the Antichrist—will bring about great loss of
life because they have an unfeeling, remorseless,
unmerciful heart like that of a wild beast.

WILL ANIMALS ATTACK THEIR TORMENTORS?

On the other hand, this could also be a very literal statement. For one thing, it strikes me that I've been reading more and more accounts lately of wild animals killing people—mountain lions in California, bears in Montana and wolves in India, rampaging elephants in Africa. What's going on?

Well, once again, nature's fragile ecosystems are being tampered with by man. And, in some misguided efforts to reverse this trend, man is also reintroducing wild animals into heavily populated areas. The combination can be deadly.

"This summer (1996) we have bears coming out of our ears," reports Kathi Green of the Colorado Division of Wildlife, regarding the complaints her department has been getting. "Usually we don't get calls about problem bears until late July. This year we received our first in April. Now we are getting 25 a day."

In Colorado, Montana and California there have been recent reports of bears eating people, destroying homes and attacking livestock. Why the change? Because, thanks to misguided environmentalism, bear hunting is a no-no. Therefore, the bears are doing the hunting. Mountain lion hunting has also been prohibited in California. Within a year, mountain lions were attacking, and sometimes killing, people. Recently wolves were reintroduced into Montana and Wyoming. I can hardly wait for the grizzly results of this madness.

But just look what's happening in India. In Banbirpur a 100-pound wolf pounced on 4-year-old Anand Kumar and carried him away by the neck. When police searched three days later all they found was the boy's head. At least 33 other children have been carried off and killed in similar fashion and 20 others seriously mauled in the same area.

A HAARP FROM HELL

There are also weapons that exist today and others in the final stages of development that can so disturb the mind of both humans and wild animals that they will be driven into insanity and, obviously, rendered quite dangerous. One version of this kind of technology is HAARP.

HAARP is a top-secret U.S. government experiment involving ionosphere heating. Already there is evidence that this project has the power to disrupt normal human thought processes, jam global communications systems, change weather patterns, adversely affect human health and impact the earth's upper atmosphere.

HAARP, according to a book by authors Jeane Manning and Dr. Nick Begich, stands for High-frequency Active Auroral Research Program. It represents the reversal of a radio telescope. Instead of receiving signals, it sends them out. It is an active test of a superpowerful radio-beam technology that can actually lift areas of the ionosphere by heating them with focused energy beams. Electromagnetic waves then bounce back to earth—with many potentially devastating effects.

Based in remote Alaska, the HAARP research station consists of 36 antennas pointed skyward, the first phase of a modular, expandable system that will become the world's most powerful radio transmitter. Government documents unearthed by the researchers for their book, *Angels Don't Play This HAARP,* reveal the project will alter the ionosphere in fundamental

ways. Unintended effects of tampering with this natural atmospheric shield could be cataclysmic, say some
scientists. Nobody is really sure how this big experiment will turn out.

"The military is going to give the ionosphere a big
kick and see what happens," says Alaskan anti-HAARP
activist Clare Zickuhr.

This is a gamble with potentially irreversible
effects that could endanger much of the human race.

So how come so few of us have heard anything
about HAARP? According to the Rocky Mountain
News, the project is one of the 10 best-kept secrets of
the U.S. government—a joint project of the Air Force,
Navy and the University of Alaska. But much of the
contracting for the project is handled by a company
called ARCO Power Technologies, Inc. (APTI), a sub-
sidiary of The Atlantic Richfield Company. APTI holds
patents for "making nuclear-sized explosions without
radiation" and "weather modification by manipulating
the ionosphere."

HAARP was deliberately placed directly under the
aurora borealis, the atmospheric glow known as the
northern lights. Its designers claim it will someday be
able to communicate with submarines, remotely sense
underground structures such as tunnels and oil
deposits, prolong the life of satellites, boost radar puls-
es and serve as an anti-missile defense shield. With
such high-stakes potentials as these, mere potential
threats to human survival will not stop its development.

The Russians have been working on similar pro-
jects for the purpose of mind and weather control and
alteration. Recently a top Russian scientist boasted of
his nation's advanced research into so-called "plasma"

weapons. The ionosphere is an active electrical shield protecting the planet from the constant bombardment of high-energy particles from space. This conducting "plasma," along with earth's magnetic field, traps the electrical plasma of space and holds it back from going directly to the surface of the planet, explains Dr. Begich.

Could HAARP actually be used for mind control? One potential military use of the HAARP system is the production of high-powered electronic oscillations that could seriously impair the brain performance of very large populations in selected regions over an extended period, says Dr. Begich.

One wonders if such a scheme might tie in with general Bible prophecies about the great deception in which the whole world accepts an Antichrist figure as God. But, more specifically, could such a weapon be the cause of the confusion cited by Zechariah on the battlefields of the last great war (Zechariah 10:5)? Or, is this one of the devices that will be used to turn ordinary men into the "wild beasts" depicted in Revelation 6:8?

When we begin to factor in all of the weapons of mass destruction and high technology that will be used in the world war, the scene described by the Apostle John begins to make more sense. There will be tremendous disruption and dislocation of natural habitats by the effects of thermonuclear, biological, chemical and HAARP-type weaponry. Is there any reason to doubt that wild animals—even domesticated pets—might turn on humans for both food and revenge?

If this is the case, then the killing done by the wild animals and God-haters will be intensely close and personal. In the first, second and third centuries, the

Roman Empire fed Christians to the wild beasts for entertainment in their coliseums. In the next few years, nonbelievers may be subjected to the same fate.

MANKIND'S INSANE RESPONSE

Mankind responds to these terrible first four judgments by launching a rampant slaughter of all persons who have come to faith in Jesus as Savior and Lord. This brings on the unleashing of mankind's greatest long-standing fear, as we will see in the next chapter.

THE SEALS OF MASS DESTRUCTION

CHAPTER FIVE

**"Behold, the day of the LORD is coming, cruel,
with fury and burning anger...The stars of
heaven and their constellations will not flash
forth their light; the sun will be dark when it
rises, and the moon will not shed its light. Thus
I will punish the world for its evil, and the
wicked for their iniquity; I will also put an end
to the arrogance of the proud, and abase the
haughtiness of the ruthless. I will make
MORTAL MAN SCARCER THAN PURE GOLD..."**

—Isaiah 13:9-12 (750 BC)

THE MOST UNREPORTED ATROCITIES

Nine Rwandan priests, three nuns slain in Zaire. ...Nigerian state security agents harass pastors. ...South Korean missionaries under fire in China. ...Myanmar's Karen Christians facing genocide. ...Hindu political parties target Christians in India. ...Proposed draft law on religion in Macedonia threatens church freedoms. ...Imprisoned pastor bailed out in Pakistan. ...Bombers, thieves attack Armenian churches in Istanbul. ...Syrian Orthodox Christian released in southeast Turkey. ...Evangelical churches in Colombia face guerrilla attacks. ...Egyptian army attacks Christian land reclamation project.

...Christian expatriate remains imprisoned in Tehran.
...Assyrian Christians murdered publicly in Iraq.
...Egyptian Christians massacred by terrorists. ...

All over the world, Christians are being persecuted and attacked for their beliefs. You might not notice it, because the secular press pays little attention. Even the American churches have been far too quiet for far too long as their brethren pay the ultimate price as believers.

From China and Vietnam and Bosnia to Algeria and Egypt and Pakistan, Christians are under fire, just as the Bible predicted they would be. And this is not completely a new phenomenon, though the 20th century has witnessed far more persecution of believers than the world has seen since the time of Rome.

A SCORE
THAT WILL BE SETTLED

A Russian presidential commission reported in 1996 that 200,000 Christian clergy were murdered under 70 years of Soviet rule—many of them by the most grotesque means imaginable, including crucifixions, scalpings and "bestial torture."

Have you ever wondered why, when it comes to executing Believers in Jesus, such horrible, bestial methods of capital punishment are used? Christians in the Roman Empire were doused in oil, impaled on poles and used as torches to light the garden parties of Rome; fed to lions and wild beasts in the gladiators' arena; used for archery and javelin practice; cut in pieces; etc. And in this matter, modern society is still the same today. There are no secular human rights activists rising to condemn the documented atrocities that have taken place all over the world, especially in Communist countries. CNN is not doing investigative reporting on them either. Why is this?

"Clergymen were crucified on churches' holy gates, shot, strangled, doused in water in winter until they froze to death," said Alexander Yakovlev, chairman of the Commission for the Rehabilitation of the Victims of Political Repression. In fact, repression against believers is more the rule than the exception. As we approach the new millennium, the world is facing unprecedented anti-Christian bigotry and persecution. The world is being rapidly polarized in attitude toward true Christians. The ugly side of mankind's fallen nature is beginning to appear, and hatred toward true Christians is surfacing in many places of power.

Why is this trend accelerating? Because it was predicted to happen shortly before the Lord's Second Coming: **"Then they will deliver you up to tribulation, and will kill you, and you will be hated by all nations on account of My name"** (Jesus in Matthew 24:9); and because, **"If the world hates you, you know that it has hated Me [Jesus] before it hated you. If you were of the world, the world would love its own. But because you are not of the world, but I choose you out of the world, therefore the world hates you...He who hates Me hates My Father also"** (John 15:18, 19 and 23).

Michael Horowitz of the Hudson Institute conducted a study of persecution of Christians throughout the world and found most of it is practiced by two forms of government—communist totalitarians and Islamic regimes. Horowitz said evangelicals and Catholics are the Jews of the 21st century and took note of the fact that few of the mainline church organizations have done anything to intercede on behalf of oppressed and persecuted believers abroad.

Pretending, however, doesn't make the situation any better. In fact, to one extent or another the Western Churches of developed nations have been shirking their responsibility for persecuted brothers and sisters in Christ for all of the 20th century. If you are the praying sort, I encourage you to stop right here—take a moment—and pray for the persecuted church. Pray for the home church movement in China where some 300 million Christians are forced underground to worship the God of the Bible. Pray for the Christians in Sudan who are sold into slavery and tortured because of their faith, and for the Coptic Christians in Egypt who are being persecuted and killed by Moslem fanatics. It's hard to believe this is happening in our world today, but it is!

HELP THE HELPLESS WHILE WE CAN

And we shouldn't stop there. If time allows, we should seek to build a political consensus in this country that will raise the price on those regimes that resort to such barbaric and inhumane practices. Instead of rewarding them with Most Favored Nation trading status, leasing them ports of call in the continental United States and accepting their massive campaign contributions, we ought to give them the left foot of fellowship.

MASS MURDER OF CHRISTIANS WILL BE POLITICALLY CORRECT

But I digress. For the persecution we are seeing in our world today, while horrifying, is but a foretaste of what is in store for believers in the near future. It is a fact, God's word tells us, that countless believers will seal their new-found testimony with martyrdom during the Tribulation.

"And when He had opened the fifth seal, I saw under the altar the souls of those who had been slain because of the word of God, and because of their testimony which they had held. And they cried with a loud voice, saying, 'How long, O Lord, holy and true, do You not judge and avenge our blood on those who dwell on the earth?' And white robes were given to every one of them; and they were told to rest for just a little while longer, until their fellow servants also and their brothers, that should be killed as they were, should be fulfilled" (Revelation 6:9-11).

It's a sobering reality that if people will not receive God's gift of salvation now, while it is still relatively easy—at least here in the United States—when the Tribulation judgment begins, it will be "so as by fire." Most of those who become believers during that period will be killed. They will be easy to identify. Why? Because the Antichrist of Rome will require that all men on earth swear total allegiance to him. All who refuse to profess this allegiance will not be given the Antichrist's special identifying mark on their forehead or hand. Without this mark, whose prefix is 666, no one will be allowed to buy, sell or hold a job. Only a believer in Jesus would have a reason not to receive this number, so therefore they will be exposed and slaughtered by the millions. Much more about this later.

COULD GLOBAL CONTROL REALLY HAPPEN?

Is such a thing possible? Are we really heading toward the kind of global government that would facilitate such drastic measures? Is all this just a little farfetched?

The fact of the matter is that the world is moving

rapidly toward a one-world system of government. Indeed, there are even plans afoot to unite all of the world's religions along the same lines as countries have been brought together in the United Nations.

In 1996, the United Nations Commission on Global Governance (yes, they really have such a commission) completed a three-year study of how to implement world government by the year 2000. The report came in the form of a 410-page book titled *Our Global Neighborhood,* published by Oxford University Press.

"It is simply not feasible for sovereignty to be exercised unilaterally by individual nation-states, however powerful," wrote Maurice Strong, former head of the U.N. Environment Program and secretary-general of the U.N. Conference on Environment and Development. "It is a principle which will yield only slowly and reluctantly to the imperatives of global environmental cooperation."

While we seldom see such candor from public officials in our newspapers, which seem to want to "protect us" from the plans of our government leaders, these kinds of statements are being made on the public record. You just have to search for them to find them. The people doing the plotting are no longer members of secret societies with weird handshakes and funny hats. They are some of our most respected diplomats and elected officials.

"Although people are born into widely unequal economic and social circumstances, great disparities in their conditions or life chances are an affront to the human sense of justice," the U.N. report continued.

It's clear reading these documents that environmental and social concerns will be the principle vehicles by which the U.N. consolidates its power. Under the plan, the U.N. Trusteeship Council would be restructured to give 23 individuals extraordinary international powers over what the report calls the "global commons."

THE SUBTLE GRAB OF GLOBAL SOVEREIGNTY

And what are the "global commons"? "The atmosphere, outer space, the oceans and the related environment and life support systems that contribute to the support of human life," says the report. In other words, virtually everything will be under global stewardship.

But what power does the U.N. really have? All existing international environmental treaties—about 300 of them—are already administered by the U.N. This new plan would simply place them under the authority of the Trusteeship Council and give the U.N. wider enforcement power.

Did you know the U.N. is closing off millions of acres of the American West? It's true. Under provisions of the 1972 World Heritage Treaty, the United States government is now required to get approval for development near World Heritage Sites. The Clinton administration has taken this very seriously and has complied to the letter with all U.N. demands.

In 1997 President Clinton designated millions of acres of national parkland in Utah as wilderness area, putting it off-limits to mining and even some tourism. All this is merely part of the U.N.'s bigger picture— "Agenda 21," a blueprint for global environmental dictatorship that calls for "re-wilding" at least half the continental United States. The premise of the whole program is that human society is a cancer on the planet and that radical surgery is required to bring it under control. The prophets of the Bible have news for these people: God is going to do some radical surgery on this planet—not the U.N.

Rep. Helen Chenoweth has it right. She points out that the U.N. plans smack of a religious worldview—*"a cloudy mixture of earth worship, pagan mysticism and folklore."* That worldview was endorsed by Interior Secretary Bruce Babbitt during an address to the National Religious Partnership for the Environment when he condemned traditional Christianity and exalted pagan nature worship.

"The U.N. is in the process of acquiring its own superlative status as the primary lawmaking entity for the world," explains Henry Lamb, founder and chairman of the Environmental Conservation Organization.

He's not the only one making such statements these days. In a book called *Bold New World,* William Knoke, founder of the Harvard Capital Group, writes: "In the 21st century, we will each retain our 'indigenous' cultures, our unique blend of tribal affiliations, some acquired by birth, others chosen freely. Many of us will live in one place for most of our lives and take pride in the local region. Yet our passion for the large nation-state, for which our ancestors fought with their blood, will dwindle to the same emotional consequences of county or province today. A new spirit of global citizenship will evolve in its place, and with it the ascendancy of global governance."

Knoke sees trading blocs such as NAFTA and the European Union as the precursors of world government.

"In each case, we are experimenting with new ways to link countries, to yield sovereignty in exchange for something more than what is lost," Knoke writes. "What happens in Europe will very much be the model for world consolidation in the 21st century, not just economically, but politically and socially as well."

Knoke says the U.N. must be armed with taxing powers, and it must maintain a world police force manned by "peacekeepers" who are "a combination of social worker, policeman, riot police and Rambo-style SWAT commandos."

THE DANGEROUS GLOBAL LEADERSHIP VACUUM

So what's holding back this Brave New World? Probably only a vacuum of leadership. Have you noticed how few strong leaders there are in the world right now? Where are the Churchills and the Reagans and the Thatchers? For that matter, where are the Stalins and the Maos? No personalities seem capable of uniting people throughout a continent and throughout a world.

The State of the World Forum, founded by Mikhail Gorbachev, has taken note of this leadership vacuum and is attempting to do something about it. In 1996, Gorbachev convened an impressive array of dignitaries and power brokers in San Francisco for a $3.5 million conference broadcast around the world.

"From the outset," he said, "I would like to suggest that we consider the establishment of a kind of global brain trust to focus on the present and the future of our civilization."

Even more to the point, Co-chairman Thabo Mbeki, executive deputy president of South Africa, said: "There will be no day of days when a new world order will come into being. Step by step and here and there, it will arrive, and even as it comes into being, it will develop fresh perspectives, discover unsuspected problems and go on to new adventures. We make bold to say that some of those new adventures will consist in what we have sought to describe—the formation of a new system of governance marked by a dynamic interaction between an empowered citizenry, national government that will have been impacted upon by the erosion and diffusion of its powers and the enhancement of global governance: *What it is that 'slouches toward Bethlehem to be born' remains to be seen."*

Students of Bible prophecy know the difference between the person born in Bethlehem and what will be born of man's misguided attempts at global government. Yet, the march toward globalism seems almost unstoppable. The groundwork is being laid today for a worldwide computer banking system that will permit one man to control the entire population of the world. Americans have shown they are not adverse to the personal identification number (PIN) that most banks require of us as secret access codes to use automated teller machines. We're being well-programmed.

Eventually, one secret number will give a person access to all of his individual needs—both at home and at work. That may sound good to some. But, of course, all information about your personal and credit habits will also be accessible to others and instantly available by computer.

Population control is here. It's only a matter of time before the slaughter of the innocents begins.

THE FIRST GLOBAL NUCLEAR EXCHANGE

As if all that weren't enough to worry about, consider what the next six verses of the Apocalypse tell us. The opening of the sixth seal introduces a tremendous earthquake. Earthquakes have always been terrifying experiences.

As I pointed out earlier in this book, experts agree that the frequency of earthquakes is increasing significantly and that "killer quakes" are happening more often than ever before. As the earth becomes more heavily populated and developed, the damage from quakes increases proportionately. Notice the death tolls from recent quakes in areas of even the most desolate parts of the world today. They're astounding! In fact, earthquakes this century have killed more than 2 million people—or half the toll of all natural catastrophes put together! But it's going to get much worse.

Professor R.A. Daly, author of *Our Mobile Earth,* says that "by far the most awful earth shock is yet to come." Seismologist Otto Nuttli of St. Louis University, and the man who pointed out the dangers of the New Madrid Fault, said a jolt like the one in 1811 "would cause a disaster whose magnitude would only be eclipsed by an all-out nuclear war." Guess what? We're going to get both.

"And I looked when He opened the sixth seal, and there was a great earthquake, and the sun became black as sackcloth of hair, and the moon became like blood; And the stars of heaven fell to the earth, even as a fig tree drops its untimely figs, when it is shaken by a mighty wind. And the atmosphere was pushed apart like a scroll when it is rolled together; and every mountain and island were moved out of their places. And the kings of the earth, along with the great men, the rich men, the chief captains, the mighty men, every slave, and every free man, hid themselves in the dens and in the rocks of the mountains, then said to the mountains and rocks, 'Fall on us, and hide us from the face of Him who sits on the throne, and from the wrath of the Lamb; for the great day of His wrath has come, and who is able to stand?" (Revelation 6:12-17).

ICBM'S, EARTHQUAKES AND NUCLEAR WINTER?

If this is an earthquake described in this sixth judgment, it will be of a magnitude never even conceived of by mankind. It will be "the mother of all earthquakes." The Greek word (σεισμος) used here actually means "a violent, catastrophic shaking, not necessarily caused by an earthquake." This root meaning, coupled with the darkening of the sun and the moon, leads me to believe that the Apostle John is describing a chain of earthquakes triggered by multiple nuclear explosions near major fault lines. Scientists have warned of the terrible repercussions of such an action—nuclear winter, which does exactly what John describes. The enormous amount of debris hurled into the atmosphere will almost blot out the sun, moon and the stars.

Apply the Apocalypse code here. John had to describe phenomena of a very advanced technical age in terms of his first-century understanding. But we now know that a worldwide nuclear war could set off a chain reaction of quakes that could leave the planet shaking as it has never shaken before. Since there has never been a great number of thermonuclear warheads set off in near proximity both in time and location, we can only theorize what possible effects an all-out nuclear exchange could cause. Certainly there is the possibility of triggering earthquakes and volcanic eruptions. There is also the possibility of igniting a chain reaction of firestorms over large areas.

I'm fascinated by weaponry. I admit it. When I was studying about nuclear weapons, I discovered that science has perfected a cobalt bomb—one of the most lethal weapons known to man. A cobalt bomb is made by placing a cobalt 59 metal around a hydrogen bomb. By this comparatively simple operation, the destructive capacity of the hydrogen bomb is doubled. The radioactive contamination of the cobalt bomb is tremendous. Scientists have dubbed it "the dirty bomb" because it produces so much fallout. This is what I believe may be pictured in Revelation 6:12.

THE NEUTRON BOMB EFFECT

There is also the neutron version of a nuclear bomb. This has been nicknamed "Dial a nuke" by the military. These nuclear bombs and shells can be pre-programmed to kill everything within a predetermined radius with an intense burst of radiation that kills every carbon-bearing life form, or living things made of flesh. They do not destroy buildings or equipment. This makes it an irresistible battlefield weapon, especially for an army facing massed troops with a great numerical superiority. Could this be why Israel has developed and built more neutron bombs of various sizes and applications than any other nation?

The second seal unleashed the initial wave of invasion into the Middle-East, which I believe without doubt will be led by Russia and a confederacy of Moslem nations of the region—incited by Iran. The prophet Ezekiel predicted this invasion would start a war that would escalate to the whole world. Twenty-five hundred years ago Zechariah the prophet described the horrible way that soldiers who invaded Jerusalem and Israel would die: "**Now this will be the plague with which the LORD will strike all the peoples who have gone to war against Jerusalem; while they stand on their feet their flesh will be consumed, their eyes consumed out of their sockets and their tongues consumed from their mouths**" (Zechariah 14:12). This is exactly the way a neutron bomb works. A soldier is hit by a burst of radiation that leaves only a skeleton within a nanosecond. How could Zechariah have known such a thing 2500 years ago? Once again, the Apocalypse code unlocks the meaning of something not understood for centuries, because the technology for such things did not exist until now.

Revelation 6:13 states, **"And the stars of the sky fell to earth, as a fig tree casts its unripe figs when shaken by a great wind..."** This word translated **star**, as previously noted, can equally mean either an asteroid or a meteor—depending on the context. But once again the Apocalypse code scenario helps us understand. I believe that the Apostle John was seeking to describe a phenomenon he had never seen and couldn't understand. I believe he witnessed the first all-out nuclear exchange between warring nations. One Inter-Continental Ballistic Missile (ICBM) with Multiple Independently-targeted Re-entry Vehicles (MIRVs) can deliver up to twelve thermonuclear warheads. (Russia even had one version of the SS-18 ICBM, code named *Satan*, that carried 30 MIRVs.) They are released in space to proceed to their different pre-programmed targets. When each warhead re-enters the earth's atmosphere they leave a fiery red trail like a flaming meteor or asteroid. The fact that John said there were many falling like unripe figs in a windstorm gives added weight to this argument. And so does the effect they cause on earth, as we will see in a moment.

However, verse 13 may also be referring to even more than ordinary ICBMs. Russia now has a weapon called a "fractional orbital bomb." It consists of a dozen or so nuclear-tipped missiles which can be fired simultaneously from an orbiting space platform. Because the missiles come straight down from the sky, they can strike several cities simultaneously with virtually no warning. When these missiles reenter the atmosphere and streak through the air they look like meteors showering the planet. The Apostle John's description of the **sun** becoming black as sackcloth and the **moon** becoming like blood could be perfectly explained by the tremendous amounts of dust, ash and debris blown into the sky by multiple nuclear bursts. The so-called "nuclear-winter" scenario would also result from there same conditions.

Think about the words chosen in verse 14: **"And the atmosphere was pushed apart like a scroll when it is rolled together."** Do you know what happens in a nuclear explosion? The atmosphere is rolled back on itself by the enormous blast forces! It's these tremendous forces of air, both initially and in the violent return into the vacuum, that cause much of the destruction of a nuclear explosion. Considering John's first-century limitations, the words in this verse paint an excellent picture of an all-out nuclear exchange. When this happens, John continues, every mountain and island will be jarred from its present position. The whole world will be shaken.

MOST UNBELIEVERS WILL GET HARDER

And what will be the reaction to these events of the Six Seals? People—even diehard atheists—will fall to their knees and beg for mercy. But notice to whom they pray—not to God, but to the inanimate rocks and mountains. There is no true repentance and seeking of the True God here—just an understandable cry for relief.

As soon as there is a lull in the catastrophes, most of the world will go back to the same old ways of unbelief. They will think the worst is over and things just have to get better. Wow, if they only knew—this is only phase one of a three-phased Apocalyptic holocaust!

Catastrophes increase in frequency and intensity on a geometric scale from here on.

THE GREAT INTERLUDE
AND INVITATION

However, first comes an interlude of grace. Everyone who earnestly seeks the Truth shall find it. Everyone who cries out to the LORD Jesus will find Him. Then He will cease being their Judge and become their Savior— for the Word of God promises, **"The SUN shall be turned into darkness, and the MOON into blood, before the coming of the great and terrible day of the LORD. And it shall come to pass that whoever calls upon the name of the LORD shall be saved"** (The Prophet Joel 2:31-32, about 835 BC).

144,000 UNSTOPPABLE WITNESSES

CHAPTER SIX

**"And this good news of the kingdom shall be
preached to the whole inhabited earth
for a witness to all the gentiles,
and then the end shall come."**

—A prophesy of Jesus, Matthew 24:14

After reading about the horrible catastrophes unleashed by the fifth and sixth Seals, you may be asking yourself the same question raised at the end of verse 17 in Revelation 6: **"Who can possibly stand up to these horrors?"** The Apocalypse, chapter 7, answers that question. Once again, it shows that even in the midst of judgment, God always pauses to offer mercy to those who will receive His gift of forgiveness through faith in Jesus. The amazing thing is that even in this time of long overdue retribution, God sees to it that the whole world hears the good news of salvation through faith in His Savior, Jesus. Even as the planet is exploding in violence, and plagued by the worst natural disasters ever experienced by man, this grace will be offered and millions will receive it.

After the six seals of judgment are opened, the eyes of some survivors on earth are opened to the truth for the first time. In this chapter, the Apostle John provides a glimpse of the powerful witness to free forgiveness through faith in the Messiah, Jesus. This will take place all during this period of unprecedented global destruction.

As is typical of these parenthetical explanatory chapters in the Apocalypse, this one begins with a flashback to the very beginning of the seven-year Tribulation period, to show that God set this grace in motion before any judgment was allowed to start.

"YOU SHALL SEEK ME AND FIND ME WHEN YOU SEARCH FOR ME WITH ALL YOUR HEART."

—A PROMISE FROM GOD ALMIGHTY (Deuteronomy 4:29)

God has never been without a witness of His salvation on this earth. Since all believers from this present age will have been suddenly and miraculously removed by the event known as the Rapture, new witnesses must be raised up immediately.

Imagine what would happen if, suddenly, in the midst of some very trying times on earth, 144,000 Israelites instantly and miraculously became devout believers in Jesus as their promised Messiah and Savior. This will occur much the same as Rabbi Saul of Tarsus was miraculously brought to faith on the road to Damascus. I don't know what will cause the conversion, other than the power of the Holy Spirit. But in multiple miraculous incidences, 144,000 Jews will be brought to faith in Jesus as the Messiah and Son of God, and will become powerful evangelists. Picture 144,000 Hebrew Billy Grahams running around the world and bringing this miraculous saving truth to a troubled and confused populace. That's just what's going to happen.

The first question you may have is: "Why are they all Jews?" First we must understand why God has a special role for the nation of Israel—the special place He has in his heart for the Jewish people, His chosen people.

That's really what most of the Bible is all about, starting with Genesis 11 and continuing uninterrupted through the Gospel of Luke. Even later New Testament books, such as Hebrews and James, have a strong Jewish emphasis. Think about it: In at least three-fourths of the Bible the focus is on the Israelite people. That should give you a pretty good clue as to the importance which they hold in the eternal purposes of God.

Remember, God called Abraham out of Assyria about 4,000 years ago. He presented him with several fantastic promises and, also, some sobering responsibilities. He promised the elderly Abraham a son—an heir who would father a unique race of people, a nation chosen and blessed in a special way by God Himself.

WHY IN THE WORLD DID GOD CHOOSE THE JEW?

And what were God's purposes in making these promises to the Jews? There were probably many, but here are four main reasons:

1. It was the Jews who had the special responsibility to receive and write down God's revelations to man. This critical mission was accomplished. Virtually every book of both the Old and New Testaments was authored by a Jew under the inspiration of God. Some argue about possible exceptions, but none has ever been proven or even argued persuasively.

2. The Jews were chosen to protect and preserve the purity of the autographed original manuscripts they had transcribed under the inspiration of God. Their success is one of the wonders of the ancient world. Think of what we all owe the Jews in gratitude for the way they accomplished this job in spite of incredible adversity, turbulence and even the destruction of their country. When the Dead Sea Scrolls were discovered in the 1940s, many "scholars" expected to see significant differences between the wording of these Scriptures which had been recorded around 200 B.C. and the earliest manuscripts we had at the time, which were over 1,100 years later. Surprise! They were virtually identical.

3. Israel was needed to provide a human family through whom the Messiah, the Savior of all mankind, could be born. Did you know there are more than 300 specific prophecies in the Old Testament about the coming of the Messiah as a humble suffering servant? The great paradox is that when He did come, the very people who had predicted the event rejected Him! They were looking for the second portrait of the Messiah predicted in the Old Testament—that of mighty conquering King and Priest, who would deliver them from their political oppressors. The religious leaders had strayed so far from the truth of the Torah that they had become self-righteous and saw no need for a humble Messiah who came to die for their sins.

After all, they reasoned, we are not sinful like the Gentiles. They opted for the glories of the Conquering Messiah King who would fulfill their fleshly desires to reign over the world as priests. They failed to see the most important fact, "There can be no crown without a Cross." This is why the Messiah had to first come and die for our sins. He will come the second time to set up His kingdom for all who have received His pardon by faith alone.

But think about the way the New Testament begins: **"These are the ancestors of Jesus Christ, a descendant of King David and of Abraham** (Matthew 1:1, TLB).

4. The Jews were selected to witness to the pagan world that there is only one true God and to show men how to know Him. The mere survival of the Jewish people—scattered for centuries, regathered and reborn as a nation in this generation—is the single greatest testimony to the truth of the Bible. The Jews remain a living witness to God's reality.

While God has a special place in His heart for the Jews, He has also allowed a national spiritual blindness to come upon them. How else can one explain the way the Gentile world accepted the simple truth of Jesus so readily, while so many Jews rejected Him? At the same time, it's important to remember that, in every generation since the first, some Jews have accepted Jesus as Messiah and Lord. In biblical terminology, these folks are referred to as **"the believing remnant."**

Despite the worldwide dispersion and persecution of the Jews from the first century through the 20th, God kept His promises of eternal blessings and will someday restore the Jews to a position of special favor. At this moment in history, it is the Church (all true believers in Jesus Christ) who enjoy God's special blessing. The drama of this shifting emphasis is told by Paul in Romans 9, 10 and 11. This would be a good time to review those Scriptures. And here's a way to understand the message: Romans 9 explains the Jews' **election**; Romans 10 reveals reasons for their **rejection**; and Romans 11 promises their national **restoration**.

God has promised never to abandon His chosen people. The divine hand of protection of the Jews during their five major wars against enemies that far outnumbered them are modern-day illustrations of how He keeps His promises. The world has witnessed the Jews' election, rejection and partial restoration in the land of Israel. We are nearing the moment in history when they will be spiritually restored as well as physically restored.

"For I don't want you, brothers, to be ignorant concerning this misery," wrote Paul in Romans 11:25, **"lest you should become wise in your own eyes, that a partial blinding has come upon Israel until the fullness of the Gentiles has been brought in."** In other words, at some point in history —very soon, I believe—God's special focus and blessing is going to shift back to the Jews. At that moment, the Jews will once again be responsible, as God's representatives, to take His message to the whole world. This mission—incomplete and seemingly impossible for the last 2,000 years—will be accomplished by the 144,000 Jewish Billy Grahams in seven years.

GOD HOLDS BACK THE STORM ...TEMPORARILY.

"After these things I saw four angels standing on the four corners of the earth, holding the four

winds of the earth, so that the wind could not blow on the earth or on the sea or on any tree. Then I saw another angel ascending from the east, having the seal of the living God; and he cried with a loud voice to the four angels, to whom it was given to hurt the earth and the sea, saying, 'Do not hurt the earth or the sea or the trees, until we have sealed the servants of our God in their foreheads'" (Revelation 7:1-3).

Angels, huh? There's been a lot of talk about angels lately. Angels are very popular. They're the in thing these days. You see books about them in all the bookstores. Movies are being made about them by the score, it seems. This generation has less trouble believing in angels than in the God who created them.

Make no mistake about it, folks. Angels are real. And they play a very important role in the predicted judgments of God on earth. But you need to understand that there are three categories of angels.

THREE ORDERS OF ANGELS

First, there are the angels of God who remained faithful to Him when Lucifer rejected God and led a rebellion against Him. Secondly, there are the angels who followed Lucifer and are still working on His behalf. Thirdly, however, is a group you seldom hear about—a group of fallen angels who are bound and imprisoned.

This last group is a particularly vicious gang that God locked up in a place called "the abyss" to await the final execution of their sentence—to be cast with Lucifer (Satan) and the other demons into the Lake of Fire (2 Peter 2:4).

Remember, angels—good or bad—have special

intelligence and powers. The four mentioned in Revelation 7, verse one apparently have been given authority over the weather conditions of the earth. Think about how even subtle changes in the world's wind patterns would radically impact on the earth's delicate ecological balance. Note that verse 2 says, **"...the four angels, to whom it was given to hurt the earth."** This harm will be upon the earth, the sea and the trees.

Have you ever considered how much damage and destruction are caused by wind? If you've ever experienced the sheer terror of a great hurricane, typhoon, dust storm, or tornado, you know what I'm talking about. If not, you may have gotten a pretty good idea by watching the movie *Twister.*

Many of the prophecies relating to this tribulation period indicate freak weather conditions and storms of unprecedented intensity and ferocity. Jesus Himself predicted that strange phenomena would occur regarding the relationship of the earth to the sun, moon and stars: **"Then there will be strange events in the skies—warnings, evil omens and portents in the sun, moon, and stars; and down here on earth the nations will be in turmoil, perplexed by the roaring seas and strange tides. The courage of many people will falter because of the fearful fate they see coming upon the earth, for the stability of the very heavens will be broken up"** (Luke 21:25–26 TLB).

It's interesting to note that scientists are already warning us that the earth's weather patterns are shifting radically. But judging from what the Bible tells us about climatological upheaval in the last days, we haven't seen anything yet.

GRACE BEFORE JUDGMENT

Before the four angels are allowed to execute their judgment of shifting wind patterns, another angel appears, coming up from the rising sun. This angel has the **"seal of the living God"** with which he empowers God's 144,000 special earthling servants (Revelation 7:2-4). What is this "seal of the living God"?

The verb "to seal" means to make an imprint in wax with a signet ring. This was done in ancient business transactions of all kinds. It was a visible mark of ownership and a guarantee of protection. The seal of God in the world today is the Holy Spirit, who empowers all believers. Look in Ephesians 1:13-14 to see that the same word, "seal," is used to describe the Holy Spirit. It's also mentioned in Ephesians 4:30, II Corinthians 1:22 and 5:5. During His earthly ministry, Jesus Himself had this special seal (John 6:27).

So, once again, the Holy Spirit will be present to give a special empowering to these 144,000 servants of God to perform their awesome mission. Note that Revelation 7:3 speaks of a visible mark on their foreheads. Remember that followers of the Antichrist will have a mark on their foreheads. You can be sure these marks will contrast sharply and clearly identify these two spiritual armies. Today you may be able to serve God—or the devil—quietly and invisibly. That won't be the case during the tribulation period.

GOD'S SPECIAL PROTECTION FOR THE 144,000

Since these servants will be marked men on earth—working directly counter to the interests of the global leader—they will be "marked" men in more than one sense of the word. They will be under constant attack by the Antichrist's forces as well as the demonic powers unleashed upon the earth. At various times they will suffer from hunger, exposure, ridicule, torture and imprisonment. But they all will be miraculously preserved to continue their witness throughout the tribulation period. At the very end, the 144,000 witnesses will stand triumphantly on Mount Zion with Jesus. Jesus refers to them as "these brothers of mine" (Matthew 25:31-46).

The way a person treats these evangelists during the Tribulation will reflect whether he is a believer in their message or not. Keep in mind, it will be extremely perilous to aid and abet them. They will no doubt be on the Antichrist's "most wanted list." But the lesson is that God's man or woman is indestructible until God is finished with him here on earth.

THE WITNESSES SELECTED

"And I heard the number of those who were sealed; and there were sealed a hundred and forty-four thousand of all the tribes of the children of Israel. Of the tribe of Judah were sealed twelve thousand. Of the tribe of Reuben were sealed twelve thousand. Of the tribe of Gad were sealed twelve thousand. Of the tribe of Asher were sealed twelve thousand. Of the tribe of Naphtali were sealed twelve thousand. Of the tribe of Manasseh were sealed twelve thousand. Of the tribe of Simeon were sealed twelve thousand. Of the tribe of Levi were sealed twelve thousand. Of the tribe of Issachar were sealed twelve thousand. Of the tribe of Zebulun were sealed twelve thousand. Of the tribe of Joseph were

sealed twelve thousand. Of the tribe of Benjamin were sealed twelve thousand" (Revelation 7:4-8).

Do you know some "scholars" argue that the 144,000 evangelists aren't necessarily Jews? It's hard to believe in light of the above passage. Nevertheless, someone will always take issue with a literal interpretation of the Bible.

But, why not? Why shouldn't they be Jews? It makes perfect sense to me. It fits in so well with the counsel of God's purposes as previously addressed. Make no mistake about it, folks. These are not Jehovah's Witnesses. They are not Mormon missionaries. They are not symbols of the Church. They are Jews—real Jews!

Now, most Jews alive today do not know which tribe they come from. But God does! And He purposely selects 12,000 from each of the twelve tribes. Now, those of you who know something about Jewish history may notice that two of the original tribes—Dan and Ephraim—are missing, and that two others are substituted in their places. Why?

Some scholars believe the tribe of Dan is missing because the Jewish Antichrist, known as the False Prophet, will be a descendant. This certainly seems to be the meaning of an ancient prophecy that Jacob gave about the tribes of Israel in the last days: **"Dan will be a serpent in the way, a venomous viper by the path, that bites the horse's heels so that his rider falls backward"** (Genesis 49:17).

Ephraim is left out because that tribe led the way in causing the civil war which first divided the ten tribes of the North from the two in the South. The tribes of Dan and Ephraim were the first to lead Israel into idolatry. Does that mean individual members of this tribe are beyond redemption? No. But none of the tribe members are given the special honor of representing God in this hour of Tribulation. Instead, the tribe of Levi is substituted for Dan, and Joseph (Ephraim's father) is substituted for Ephraim.

REVIVAL TIME!

"After this I looked, and behold, a great multitude, which no man could number, of all nations, and kindreds, and peoples, and tongues stood before the throne, and before the Lamb, clothed with white robes, and palms in their hands, and cried with a loud voice, saying, 'Salvation is of our God who sits upon the throne, and of the Lamb" (Revelation 7:9-10).

The effectiveness of the evangelism during the Tribulation is overwhelming. What a revival! It's enough to make a Southern Baptist evangelist's mouth water!

It's almost impossible for us—living in the free world, still relatively unfettered by persecution—to appreciate what the converts of the 144,000 will have to endure because of their faith. The fact that, later, they are pictured standing before the throne of God in white robes during the Tribulation confirms that they all faced a death sentence and were martyred for their belief in Christ.

A TIME OF PRAISE!

"And all the angels stood around the throne, and about the Elders and the four Living Beings, and fell before the throne on their faces, and worshiped God, saying, 'Amen! Blessing, and

glory, and wisdom, and thanksgiving, and honor, and power, and might is of our God forever and ever. Amen" (Revelation 7:11-12).

Here's John's first-hand account of a remarkable scene! At the center of everything was the throne of God. Closest to it were the four Living Beings, and surrounding them and the throne were the 24 enthroned Elders.An unspecified number of angels encircled them all, and when they saw the great multitude of martyred Tribulation saints waving their palm branches and praising God, they fell on their faces before the throne and worshiped Him. Don't you just love that!

IDENTITY OF THE MULTITUDE

"And one of the Elders answered, saying to me, 'Who are these who are clothed in white robes? And from where did they come?' And I said unto him, 'Sir, you know.' And he said to me, 'These are they who came out of the Great Tribulation, and have washed their robes, and made them white in the blood of the Lamb. Therefore they are before the throne of God, and serve Him day and night in His temple: and He who sits on the throne shall dwell among them. They shall hunger no more, neither thirst any more; neither shall the sun beat down on them, nor any heat. For the Lamb who is in the midst of the throne shall feed them, and shall lead them unto living fountains of waters; and God shall wipe away all tears from their eyes' " (Revelation 7:13-17).

It reminds me of what the prophet Isaiah said— that any "robes of righteousness" that men weave from their own good deeds are nothing more than filthy, soiled rags (Isaiah 64:6). But these martyred saints took their soiled robes and washed them in the redeeming blood of our Passover lamb—Jesus, and they came out white enough for the presence of God!

God graciously rewards these persecuted children of His with the new, immortal bodies which all believers will eventually receive. Notice what an improvement they are over the old ones. Night and day they serve, but they don't get tired. No more hunger, no more thirst, no more discomfort from the heat or cold; and God Himself shall wipe away every tear. This is the state all believers will experience some day! Personally, I can't wait. And I'm glad I won't be here to live through what hellish nightmare these heroes must endure during the Tribulation.

CHAPTER SEVEN

FOUR TRUMPETS OF ECOLOGICAL DEATH

CHAPTER SEVEN

"The heavens will pass away with a great noise,
and the elements will melt with fervent heat;
both the earth and the works
that are in it will
be burned up."
—2 Peter 3:10

OUR GOVERNMENT'S CHOICE TO BE DEFENSELESS AGAINST NUKES

Do you know what the United States would do if attacked by nuclear missiles? Pray. That's right. I'm all in favor of prayer, of course. But that would be our only option. We are defenseless against an incoming attack by even one intercontinental ballistic missile today—and for the foreseeable future.

Why? Because our politicians have sold us out. The federal government's primary responsibility, of course, is to provide for the common defense of its citizenry. It's not to mail out welfare checks. It's not to confiscate our firearms. It's not even to educate our children. It's to protect us from external threat. Failure to do so is a betrayal of the Congressional oath. Current congressional attitudes and actions, or should I say inaction, on this issue border on criminal negligence at worst and outright stupidity at best.

But it's been a long time since the U.S. government had its priorities straight. So, one day, unless things change in Washington, we will be faced with the inevitable nuclear missile attack. Even if the attack is a single missile from a single rogue nation or fanatical group, we will have no defense, and hundreds of thousands of citizens will die a horrible death needlessly.

Is this really a possibility? Our intelligence agencies tell us it's a certainty. It's not a question of "if," it's a question of "when."

In the old days, the only real enemy we faced in the world was the Soviet Union. While Russia is still an adversary to contend with—particularly in the nuclear arena—things have gotten much more complicated. The "nuclear club" has expanded its membership over the last 20 years from six to 13. There are the "good guys"—like Great Britain, Israel and France—and a lot of unpredictable potential enemies, such as Russia, China, North Korea, Byelorus, Ukraine, Kazakhstan, India, Pakistan and South Africa. Then there are some really bad guys out there who are still trying to join the club—Iran, Libya, Iraq and Syria, to name a few. Iraq was 18 months away from acquiring the bomb when the Gulf War started, according to United Nations inspectors. In addition, Iran has already purchased, according to my sources, at least three nuclear warheads on the black market.

By the year 2000, U.S. intelligence sources say, as many as 24 Third World nations will have acquired ballistic missiles and half of those may have nuclear capability. The rest, though, will certainly have biological and chemical warheads that can cause quite a bit of mayhem.

With all that to look forward to, it's important for Americans to know that there is no way we can stop even one ballistic missile fired at the United States. Worse yet, there is no program under way to reduce that vulnerability. In fact, President Clinton recently negotiated a deal with Russia's Boris Yeltsin that reduces our ability even to research missile defense!

With all this in mind, let's take a look at what the Apocalypse tell us about a future global conflict.

As we've seen already, the horrors of the first five seals of the Apocalypse seem to be the inevitable results of what will happen when men's evil natures are totally unrestrained. The sixth seal then unleashes a worldwide holocaust and is God's judgment for the persecution of His saints. But the worst is yet to come...

THE SHOCK OF SILENCE AND AN OFFER OF GRACE

"And when He had opened the seventh seal, there was silence in heaven for about a half an hour. Then I saw the seven angels who stood before God, and they were given seven trumpets. Then another angel came and stood at the altar, having a golden censer; and there was given to him much incense, so that he might offer it with the prayers of all the saints upon the golden altar which was before the throne. And the smoke of the incense, which came with the prayers of the saints, ascended up before God out of the angel's hand. And the angel took the censer, and filled it with fire from the altar, and cast it upon the earth: and there were voices, and thunderclaps, and lightnings, and an earthquake. And the seven angels who had the seven trumpets prepared themselves to sound" (Revelation 8:1-6).

In verse one of this chapter, we read of an eerie silence in heaven just after the seventh seal is opened and before its judgment is released. This silence is awesome in its significance and stands in stark contrast to the joyous sounds of Elders and angels crying their praises in previous chapters. This half an hour pause might be called "the lull before the storm," because the seventh seal, which has just been opened, will bring the most terrible judgments yet. I'm sure the enormity of what is about to take place causes even God to pause and soberly assess what must be done to His errant creature, man.

The seven angels who stand in the presence of God are real personalities—not just figments of John's imagination or symbols. The Bible indicates that angels are grouped in clearly defined ranks, much as in a military command structure. The highest of all angelic beings are these seven "archangels" from the order of cherubim who stand in the presence of God. These are the ones who will announce with trumpet blasts God's next seven judgments on the earth. These seven trumpet judgments are all unleashed by the seventh seal.

A BOWL OF PRAYERS

But before they can blow their trumpets to begin the judgments, "another angel" appears on the scene. He stands at the altar holding a golden censer filled with a special kind of incense—the prayers of saints. These He offers to God.

You might wonder why I capitalized that last "He."

While many good Bible scholars believe that the "other angel" here at the altar is simply another high-ranking angel, I believe that it is none other than Christ Himself functioning in His ministry of High Priest. The golden censer was used only in the Holy of Holies by the high priest in the ritual of prayer. It was this prayer-offering function of the coming Messiah which was portrayed by the Old Testament altar of incense. Jesus is the antitype of which this was a type.

After Christ finishes offering the prayers of the saints to the Father, He fills the golden censer with fire from the altar and throws it to the earth. The earth erupts with thunder, lightning, and an earthquake. None of these things is intended to destroy anyone, but rather to warn the people on earth of the approach of additional judgments.

It's important to see that God seeks to extend the interlude of quietude as long as He can. He will give men more than adequate opportunity to think over the sixfold judgments which the world has just experienced. He'll wait eagerly for them to turn in repentance to Jesus. You see, God always proceeds reluctantly toward judgment.

However, the remaining judgments of the trumpets and bowls are a direct answer to the prayers of the martyred saints for justice. These judgments will occur in shorter intervals as the end of the Tribulation draws closer.

THE KEY TO THE TRUMPETS

Remember, again, that the Book of Revelation is John's firsthand account of what he saw and experienced when he was taken up to heaven. How difficult it must have been for him with his first-century orientation to find adequate descriptive words to verbalize the incredible things he viewed. Even 60 years ago the things described in the Apocalypse were so far beyond man's comprehension that no one dreamed they could happen apart from supernatural intervention.

But now such things as the Apostle John described are not only possible, but could happen within 30 minutes. There are already enough nuclear-tipped missiles on station and ready for launch to do everything predicted in this chapter. Dr. W.H. Pickering of Cal Tech confirmed this when he warned, *"In half an hour the East and the West could destroy civilization."*

Although I certainly believe God can cause every miracle in the Book of Revelation without the aid of man, I personally believe that the enormous environmental catastrophes described in this chapter are the direct result of nuclear weapons. In actuality, man inflicts these judgments on himself. God simply steps back and removes His restraining influence on man's fallen nature, allowing him to do what comes naturally. In fact, if the Book of Revelation had never been written, some astute 20th century person might well predict these very catastrophes within this generation. And, of course, many who don't believe the Book of Revelation, or who are unfamiliar with it, are doing just that. If you doubt this, just count the number of catastrophe films and TV series the secular media has produced in the last few years.

FIRST TRUMPET:
The End Of Grain
And A Third Of Trees

"The first angel sounded, and there followed hail and fire mixed with blood, and they were cast

upon the earth; and the third part of trees was burnt up, and all green grass burnt up" (Revelation 8:7).

To John's eyes, unfamiliar with intercontinental ballistic missiles, the holocaust he witnessed looked like "hail and fire, mixed with blood" blasted all through the atmosphere.

The devastation described in this first judgment of the second series of "sevens" is enormously greater than any in the "seal" series of judgments. This sort of firestorm, that devastates such large portions of continents, would have to be caused by a massive nuclear exchange between nations like Russia, USA, Israel, UK, France and—to a lesser degree—Iran, Pakistan and Libya.

RELATING SEQUENCES AND CONNECTIONS TO OTHER BIBLE PROPHECIES

The timing of the Russian-Muslim confederacy's invasion of Israel and parts of North Africa—predicted by the Prophets Ezekiel, Daniel and Joel—fits perfectly with this series of Trumpet judgments. The counterattack, launched by the reborn Roman Empire in Europe, supported by the U.S. and other western nations, will provoke a desperation move by Russia. They will probably launch more than 60 ICBMs and submarine-based missiles at Europe, USA and Canada to stop the counterattack from cutting off their supply lines and isolating them. The moment the Russian-Muslim invasion of Israel and the Middle East begins, all nations in the "nuclear missile club" will re-program their ICBMs to "launch-on-warning" status. That means missles will be pre-set to launch as soon as a satellite detects an enemy missile launch. So, ICBMs launched by both sides will probably pass each other in space as Western missiles are targeted toward Russia, Iran and Lybia. This is the "launch or lose them" mentality. This has always been terrifying to those involved in the actual program because of so much possibility of error.

THE HORRORS NUKES CAN CAUSE

The scope of the damage that will be done to our planet is almost unbelievable—unless you are knowledgeable about the anticipated aftermath of a major nuclear missile exchange. As I wrote earlier, scientists really don't know the full extent of lethality and destruction that many thermonuclear warheads exploded in close proximity of time and locations would produce. At present, thank God, it's all theoretical. But one of the effects all nuclear scientists seem to agree upon is a limited chain reaction that would produce enormous areas of fire. Several theorize that 20 to 30 thermonuclear warheads detonated in close proximity of time and space in mid-America could cause a firestorm that would sweep from the Appalachians to the Rocky Mountains. A firestorm could also be caused from Eastern Europe to the Steppes of the Ural Mountains, and from the North Sea to the Caucasus Mountains.

The detonation of nuclear weapons has a number of powerful effects, including the immediate release of X-ray radiation energy followed by thermal radiation, atmospheric blast and the subsequent lethal dispersal of longer-term radiation fallout, which is carried in dust from the bomb and residue from a crater.

The explosive components of a typical thermonuclear one-megaton weapon instantly rise to temperatures of several million degrees and create a fireball of heat and radiation, usually culminating in fallout. An explosion in the atmosphere also causes a shockwave of compressed atmosphere that travels about one-half mile in two seconds. This causes enormous over-pressure. Here the first shock wave meets a reactive reflection. Thermal radiation also occurs, and humans and animals within a radius of 12 miles from ground zero (where the bomb detonated) can be cremated. Buildings will suffer damage mainly from explosion and fire.

For the survivors of a nuclear blast, the world will be nothing like what we know today. Dr. Jack Geiger, a professor of community medicine at City College of New York and an expert on the effects of nuclear war, has described what it is like to be caught in the middle of one of these man-made storms. The following calculations are based on a 750-kiloton to one-megaton hydrogen bomb:

"First," he says, "would come a flash seven times brighter than the sun. Those within a 35-mile radius who were looking in that direction would be blinded—some only temporarily." A few moments later would come the heat flash—several times the temperature of the sun's surface—which is 11,000 degrees Fahrenheit. Those from 5 to 15 miles away from the blast's center would receive third-degree burns on all exposed skin. Anyone in the open within up to 5 miles of ground zero would be virtually cremated.

The blast itself would level and ionize everything within a one-and-a-half-mile radius of ground zero with a force 20 to 50 times the atmosphere's pressure. Geiger estimates that 45 percent of Chicago's 6.6 million people would die within a day if such a bomb struck the city on a typical working day. An estimated

65 percent of the city's hospital beds would be destroyed, and only one in six doctors would be able to function professionally.

"Surviving doctors would have to face almost every conceivable type of injury"—ranging from severe burns to fractures to crushed bodies. Soon, all of the really seriously injured would be dead because electricity failures and lack of skilled personnel would rule out the use of technically complex hospital equipment and procedures. Most casualties would need the Intensive Care Units of hospitals to survive, but these would be ineffective because of the loss of electrically powered breathing machines and vital function monitors for heart, pulse, fever and kidneys. There would be no MRIs or X-rays, which are imperative for effective diagnosis and treatment. Even less seriously injured patients would die within 24 to 36 hours. Critical medicines such as antibiotics, heart and blood pressure medicines, etc., would either be lost in the blast or used up quickly.

Only then would impact of radiation sickness begin to play a role—hundreds of thousands more would die in a matter of days and a few weeks. Medical problems stemming from cleanup of thousands of corpses alone would be devastating. Sanitation would be overwhelmed and plagues of a number of the new drug-resistant super-strain diseases would break out. The lack of uncontaminated drinking water would soon cause tens of thousands more to die. And that's just a glimpse of the situation in one city hit by a moderate-size nuclear warhead. But imagine this on a worldwide scale!

JUDGMENTS MEASURED IN THIRDS

Sometimes the trumpet judgments are referred to as "the judgment of global thirds," since one-third the planet's essential things are obliterated by them. If you've ever been in a forest fire you can imagine the terror of watching one-third of all the trees on earth go up in smoke. Think of the famine that will occur when all of the grasses and grains are incinerated by firestorms. Remember, grain is grass, too. No more wheat, rice, oats or barley. That means no more cattle or other grazing animals. Most beef cattle, milk cows, sheep, goats, pigs, chickens, turkeys, etc., would die of starvation, radiation or poisoned water within days.

With this massive loss of vegetation will come rapid soil erosion, floods and mudslides. Air pollution will be immense; the smoke of the fire will fill the entire atmosphere. The remaining vegetation will be unable to adequately absorb the hydrocarbons from automobiles and industry. The present overstrained delicate balance of ecology will be thrown into a catastrophic breakdown with ominous, unpredictable results.

Notice that God continues to be merciful even in the midst of this awful judgment. He leaves two-thirds of the greenery untouched. But, nevertheless, the remaining population refuses to change its mind about God's offer of salvation through faith in Jesus as their sin-bearer. They refuse to repent and receive a free pardon already purchased for them by the Son of God's voluntary death in their place. They refuse to dare and pray, "God, if this is true, please help me to believe and receive the gift of pardon you purchased for me."

THE SECOND TRUMPET: A Third Of The Ocean Dies

"And the second angel sounded, and something like a great mountain burning with fire was cast into the sea; and the third part of the sea became blood; and the third part of the creatures which were in the sea, and had life, died; and the third part of the ships were destroyed" (Revelation 8:8–9).

THE MOTHER OF ALL NUCLEAR NAVAL BATTLES

Notice that this verse specifies "something like a great mountain burning with fire." Again, John describes this phenomenon in terms of how it looked to him. This is probably either an enormous meteor or, more likely, a number of H-bombs. A hydrogen or thermonuclear bomb exploded under the ocean looks like a huge flaming mountain erupting out of the sea. In addition to destroying one-third of all marine vessels, the "flaming mountain" will wipe out one-third of all marine life, turning the sea crimson with the blood of the dead.

Why would such a weapon be fired into the ocean? Simple. Today, naval power, especially super nuclear submarines with ICBM launch capability, is seen as the future of warfare. Remember, Russia and the United States, still the two great nuclear powers, each have more than 100 nuclear-powered submarines capable of firing intercontinental ballistic missiles with multiple thermonuclear warheads. The Russian Typhoon class nuclear submarines are the largest, fastest, stealthiest, deepest-diving and deadliest in the world. Each one carries as standard ordinance twenty ICBMs with ten warheads each. That's 200 warheads that can turn 200 large cities into vast devastated cemeteries. These can be launched from under water and hit 95% of our major population centers in less than 8 minutes from launch.

China is buying and building these types of submarines as fast as she can. You can't very well stop your enemy from launching nuclear missiles at you without doing something about those submarines. China openly declares that it expects to be the naval power of the Pacific by the year 2015.

Iran is buying nuclear-missile-capable submarines from Russia as well. Coupled with their headlong dash toward nuclear missile capability, this should be recognized as a clear and apparent danger for the whole world, especially for Israel and the USA. With religiously fanatical leaders believing their greatest service for Allah is to die a martyr in holy war and soon to be holding their finger over a nuclear missile trigger, the whole world is in danger. One miscalculation could set the planet at risk, and possibly trigger a world conflict.

So if a nation knew it was about to be attacked by missiles fired from a submerged undetected submarine, the only way to destroy the threatening submarines in time would be to set off massive thermonuclear blast under water so that the explosive buildup of pressure would crush the submarine. It would be like a gigantic depth bomb, much like the one still used with conventional explosives.

Modern navies today from the nuclear-possessing nations have devastating nukes adapted for naval use. There are nuclear-tipped missiles that are fired from a ship at a ship. There are virtually no effective countermeasures. An aircraft can fire the deadly nuclear-tipped missile from 150 miles away. There is virtually no escape from these weapons. The same is true of nuclear armed torpedoes. There are naval adaptations of nuclear armed cruise missiles, ballistic missiles—for both surface and sub-surface launch.

THE THIRD TRUMPET SOUNDS:
A Third Of All Fresh Water Poisoned

"And the third angel sounded, and a great star [ασρηρ μεγας] **fell from heaven, burning like a torch, and it fell on a third of the rivers and on the springs of waters; and the name of the star is called wormwood** [translated Chernoble in the Ukrainian Bible]; **and a third of the waters became wormwood; and many men died from** [ek = from the source of] **the waters, because they were made poison"** (Revelation 8:10–11).

This is a difficult verse to decode and interpret. The Greek word translated **star** can literally mean "a star, an asteroid or a meteor." It is used a few times in a metaphorical sense to mean a mighty angelic being. It is, however, difficult to see how the single star falls upon a third of the freshwater rivers, lakes and ponds of the whole planet. Whatever this is, it poisons a third of all fresh water on earth. The great numbers who die do so as a direct result of drinking the polluted water.

This could be referring to some sort of an asteroid or meteor largely composed of frozen poisonous liquid chemicals that defrost with the hyper speed entry into the earth's atmosphere. Large chunks break off and are scattered over half of the earth's surface so that when melted the poisonous chemicals pollute the fresh waters.

However, I believe it is symbolic of more ICBM

warheads streaking flaming sparks as they re-enter the atmosphere. These warheads could be loaded with both nuclear and deadly chemicals together. I solve the problem of only one falling star being described by the fact that a single sword is often used to symbolize the entire weaponry of warring armies.

Certainly, radioactive, radiated debris could also poison fresh water as the nuclear fallout begins to fall in mass over the planet. With no fresh water to drink in a third of the earth, tens of thousands will die of thirst.

FOURTH TRUMPET SOUNDS: All Light From Outer Space Diminished By A Third

"And the fourth angel sounded and a third of the sun and a third of the moon and a third of the stars were smitten so that a third of them might be darkened and the day might not shine for a third of it, and the night in the same way" (Revelation 8:12).

THE FIRST NUCLEAR WINTER

With the massive amounts of debris floating in the atmosphere from the many nuclear explosions coupled with the smoke and soot from the burning of millions of trees, most of the light from outer space will be blocked out.

The impact of this upon agriculture is beyond accurate calculation at this time, but it will be enormously destructive. Most of the farming on earth will be devastated. Millions will die of the ensuing famine. The human body and health will be greatly affected by the lack of nourishing food, adequate fresh water, massive pollution and radiation in the air, much colder temperatures, and the outbreak of many super strains of infectious deceases due to the breakdown of sanitation and undernourished masses of people with lowered immune systems.

The impact of all these enormous tragedies in such a short space of time upon mankind's' emotional stability will be unimaginable. Hundreds of thousands will suffer complete mental breakdowns. Only those who turn in faith to the Lord Jesus Christ will be enabled to cope with such soul-wrenching tragedy. Virtually every individual and every family will suffer the loss of loved ones under horrific circumstances.

AND JUST WHEN YOU THOUGHT THINGS COULDN'T POSSIBLY GET WORSE... —THE THREE WOES COME!

"And I looked, and I heard an eagle flying in midheaven, saying with a loud voice, 'Woe, woe, woe to those who dwell on the earth, because of the remaining blasts of the trumpet of the three angels who are about to sound!'" (Revelation 8:13).

Whatever the eagle symbolizes, it is a means of mass communication that gets through to warn all the inhabited earth about the catastrophe horrors that are about to be unleashed on the particular group mentioned seven times in the Apocalypse as **"those who dwell upon earth."** This class of people are contrasted with **"those who dwell in heaven,"** and are apparently unbelievers. The original Greek suggests that they don't just live on earth, they actively and continuously cling to the things of this earth with its world system fashioned in defiance of God.

Since the woes are not addressed to the believers of this time, it implies that they are somehow specially protected. In light of the magnitude of the judgments already studied, there would not be a believing remnant left on earth apart from some kind of divine protection.

The fifth and sixth trumpets will bring even greater judgments than yet seen. The Asian factor is about to be introduced in these judgments. Then the seventh Trumpet opens the final series of judgments called the golden bowls or vials. These will leave the planet so devastated that, apart from divine intervention, it will no longer support life.

Why wait to decide about the free offer of Jesus, until you are left behind to suffer through this terrible period?

CHAPTER EIGHT

THE GREAT ASIAN INVASION

CHAPTER EIGHT

" 'Release the four [fallen] angels who are bound at the great river Euphrates.' So the four angels, who had been prepared for the hour and day and month and year, were released to kill a third of mankind. Now the number of the army [raised by the four fallen angels] was two hundred million."
—The Apocalypse Revelation 9:14–16

THE DREADED SHOWDOWN BETWEEN EAST AND WEST IS LAUNCHED

When this great Chinese-led Asian force moves westward, war will escalate throughout the world. In this chapter, the 200 million Asian troops are assembled and start toward the raging war in the Middle East. At the time of this chapter (Apocalypse chapter 9), the Russian-led Muslim forces are in serious jeopardy of annihilation by the Roman Antichrist-led armies of the West. **"The kings of the east"** seize this moment as the best opportunity to launch an "all-or-nothing-at-all" showdown with the Roman Antichrist for control of the world. The Asian army does not actually reach the Middle East until the events of chapter 16 of the Apocalypse.

THE BATTLE PLAN OF ARMAGEDDON

I have sought to identify the various leaders and nations by notes in brackets. Read this carefully and you will be amazed how we are already set up for just this sort of conflict. The text of Daniel's prophecy is in the bold script.

"**At the time of the end the king of the South** [Muslim forces] **shall attack him** [the False Prophet in Israel] ; **and the king of the North** [Russian leader with his army] **shall come against him** [False Prophet] **like a whirlwind, with chariots, horsemen, and with many ships; and He** [Russian leader] **shall enter the countries, overwhelm them, and pass through.**

"**He** [the Russian] **shall also enter the Glorious Land** [Israel], **and many countries shall be overthrown; but these shall escape from his hand; Edom, Moab, and the prominent people of Ammon** [nation of Jordan]. **He** [the Russian] **shall stretch ·out his hand against the** [surrounding] **countries, and the land of Egypt shall not escape.**

"**He shall have power over the treasures of gold and silver, and over all the precious things of Egypt; also the sons of Put** [Libya, Tunisia, Algeria, Morocco, Mauritania] **and the sons of Cush** [the Black Africans] **shall follow at his heels.**

"**But news from the east** [the Chinese-led Asians]

and the north [Roman-led forces of the West] **shall trouble him** [Russian leader]; **therefore he shall go out with great fury to destroy and annihilate many** [mostly Israelis].

"**And he shall plant the tents of his palace** [Russian leader's HQ] **between the seas** [Dead and Mediterranean Seas] **and the glorious holy mountain** [Temple Mount]; **yet he shall come to his end, and no one will help him**" (Daniel 11:40-45 NKJV).

The actual sequence of movement and identification of powers involved in this war are predicted in the above prophecy. The Russian and Muslim armies initially launch a coordinated two-prong attack from the north and south of Israel. The Russian commander sweeps through the strategic land bridge that begins at Istanbul and continues southward to the Suez canal. This strategic land bridge connects the continents of Europe, Asia and Africa. Israel is right at the center of the bridge, which is why so many wars have been fought back and forth over her.

This war will actually begin because of the long-smoldering dispute between the Jews and the Muslims over who owns old Jerusalem and the Temple Mount, according to Zechariah 12:2-3. The Jews believe it is their holiest place because it is the only acceptable place on earth where they are authorized by God to build the center of worship—the Temple.

The Muslims hold the same 35 acres as their third holiest place because they believe that Muhammad ascended to heaven from the great rock underneath the Dome of the Rock Mosque that stands there. This issue has become the focal point of the 4,000-year-old hatred of Isaac and his descendants by his half brother Ishmael and his descendants.

This battle plan seems to indicate that the Russian commander double-crosses many of the Muslim nations, including Egypt. Perhaps they are nations that will not go along with Iran's fanatical brand of Islamic Fundamentalism.

The Russian commander, while in Egypt, prepares to establish some sort of hegemony over Africa with the help of some African Muslim nations from the ancient tribes of Cush and Put. But at this time, news from the **east** and the **north** troubles him. The Russian leader, positioned in Egypt, learns of the mighty Asian army assembling in the East, obviously, to attack his rear eastern flank. Likewise, the troubling news from his **north** is Europe. This refers to the assembled Roman-led Western forces preparing in Europe to counterattack and cut off his vital supply lines, then to isolate the entire Russian-Muslim army.

In response to these two deadly threats, the Russian-Muslim force retreats back to Israel and sets up command HQs on the Temple Mount in Jerusalem. These forces try to annihilate the Jews as they do this.

Now this war actually began with the opening of the second seal in chapter six. By the time the Asian army reaches the Euphrates river, the Roman Antichrist's forces will have totally destroyed the Russian forces, and also the remnant of the Iranian-led Muslim forces.

Even demonic power helps facilitate this largest-of-all-time army's rapid advance into the Middle East. The mighty Euphrates River, the recognized boundary-barrier between East and West for ages past, will be supernaturally dried up to facilitate the rapid march of this Oriental juggernaut, according to The Apocalypse 16:12.

THE GIANT OF ASIA HAS AWAKENED

When John made the prophecy of 200 million Asian soldiers invading Israel to take on the armies of the West, which will be led by the revived Roman Empire, there were not 200 million people in the world.

Such a scenario must have sounded like a pipe dream even as little as 50 years ago. Though China was surely the most populated nation on the face of the earth, it was a sleeping giant—retarded technologically, economically and militarily. Today, all that has changed. Now China is poised to become the largest economy in the world in the early part of the 21st century—some major economic experts predict it will happen before the year 2000. With an unprecedented closer relationship to Russia and Japan than it has ever had in its history, it is becoming a high-tech military superpower. And with its 1.2 billion people, it represents the only nation even close to being able to mobilize a force of that size. But China announced a few months ago (1997) that they can now raise an army of 352 million soldiers. This means they could send 200 million to invade the Middle East and still have 152 million soldiers in reserve to defend the motherland.

BLATANT THREATS FROM A GROWING MENACE

Not surprising then that the totalitarians in Beijing have become so bellicose of late—illegally closing the Taiwan Strait, launching test missiles near the island of Taiwan and conducting war games designed to intimidate the inhabitants of the independent Western-oriented nation. Chinese officials also reminded the United States that they were capable of lobbing nuclear warheads on Los Angeles should America "interfere" in its "internal affairs." One high-ranking Chinese officer answered a U.S. official about our efforts to support Taiwan's right to be free. He said, "I don't really think you would be willing to lose Los Angeles over Taiwan."

According to CIA sources, China has also begun supplying technicians and equipment for a plutonium-reprocessing plant in Pakistan, a development that will assist Islamabad in its longtime effort to build an arsenal of smaller nuclear weapons—those capable of being delivered by missile or aircraft. Pakistan's 300-megawatt nuclear plant at Chashma will soon provide, according to one U.S. source, "one-stop shopping for nuclear war, courtesy of the Chinese."

China is also helping Iran with its nuclear arms program, according to a secret U.S. intelligence report. In April 1997, Chinese technicians began building a new uranium plant near Esfahan that will allow Tehran to make fissionable material for warheads. Iran has made building nuclear weapons one of its highest military priorities and should be able to produce such arms by the year 2000. A month earlier, Iran received a shipment of five Chinese Houdong fast-attack patrol boats armed with C-802 anti-ship cruise missiles that could help the Iranian navy close down the Strait of Hormuz at the south end of the Persian Gulf. Ships carrying 90 percent of Japan's oil and 60 percent of Western Europe's pass this strategic strait.

RECENT RUSSIA-CHINA PACT OPENS DEADLY ARSENAL

One factor that has allowed China to become more aggressive abroad is its new cozy relationship with longtime adversary Russia. In late April, China, Russia and three former Soviet republics in Central Asia—

Kazakhstan, Tajikistan and Kyrgyzstan—entered into an ominous non-aggression pact aimed at building a powerful regional military and economic alliance.

But an even better indicator of China's character is its continuation—even escalation—of some of the world's most hideous human rights abuses. China not only jails its political dissidents, it also works them to death in slave-labor camps. Some estimates by human rights organizations suggest a third of all China's exports are made, at least in part, by such forced labor.

THE SLAUGHTER OF THE INNOCENT

Human Rights Watch and the Population Research Institute have documented widespread starvation, medical malpractice and staff abuse throughout China's system of state-run orphanages—dubbed "children's gulags" by some observers. Such conditions are maintained as part of an official policy aimed at eliminating unwanted infants of all kinds, but particularly females and males with any kind of physical or mental defect. It is really an extension of China's one-child policy that routinely results in forced abortions and termination of pregnancies for purposes of sex selection. Abandoned girls are said to account for 90 percent of the inmate populations at Chinese orphanages. Of those that enter the institutions, 90 percent die there within a short time—usually of dehydration and malnutrition.

So what is the West doing about such atrocities? How is the United States responding to the increasing threat posed by China? Well, U.S. officials have issued mild protests. But at the same time, U.S. government policy continues to reward China as a "most-favored-nation" trading partner, a policy that permits technology transfers that have led to a breathtakingly rapid military modernization.

Could this have anything to do with the massive campaign contributions the Chinese have funneled— legally and illegally—into the coffers of some of our most powerful politicians? Is China literally buying us off? The evidence for such a notion is becoming increasingly hard to ignore.

In early 1997, a Chinese shipping firm accused of smuggling 2,000 AK-47 assault rifles for the People's Liberation Army into the United States received help from the White House in securing a lease to a historic U.S. Navy base in California. The administration claimed the deal will create 600 jobs in the Long Beach area and increase trade. But some in Congress believed security and safety issues were not taken seriously.

Just the year before, COSCO, the shipping company with close ties to the Chinese Communist government, was caught transporting guns which were intended for California street gangs. It was a COSCO ship with mechanical problems that plowed into a crowded boardwalk in New Orleans in 1996, injuring 116 people.

U.S. EXAMPLE LEADS OTHER NATIONS TO FOLLOW THE SAME FOOLISHNESS

Keep in mind that all Chinese businesses are, to one extent or another, mere extensions of the Chinese totalitarian Communist government. Can you imagine the idea of allowing the Chinese—clearly the United States' biggest foreign policy concern for the foreseeable future—to operate a naval base on the mainland U.S. ? It's happening. But it's still hard to believe that a U.S. administration could be so strategically shortsighted. Some have charged the deal amounts to treason.

The rest of the world is taking notice of the way the U.S. is capitulating to the Chinese. So it should surprise no one that longtime U.S. ally South Korea is now considering a major shift in foreign policy in which it would align itself with China, a staunch supporter of North Korea. Seoul is making the advances because of its doubts about the durability of its alliance with the United States and as a way of wedging itself between China and North Korea. South Korea is one of the continent's leading economic and military powers.

CHINA GETS RUSSIAN HELP

For 40 years during the Cold War, U.S. and European strategic planners feared one development more than any other—a strong alliance between Russia and China. Today, the Cold War may be over. The world may be at relative peace. Communism, they tell us, is dead. Yet, quietly and without fanfare, the West's worst nightmare has become a reality.

Russia, a declining superpower with one of the world's largest nuclear stockpiles, and China, a rising economic behemoth with a growing arsenal, have teamed up to form what they call a "strategic partnership" for the 21st century, reminding those familiar with Biblical prophecy that these two nations will be involved in invasions of the Middle East during the last great war on Earth.

In 1996, Russian First Deputy Prime Minister Alexei Bolshakov, on a six-day mission to China, signed major military and economic cooperation agreements. The talks included three days of discussions between Russian and Chinese military leaders. Curiously, the meetings went virtually unnoticed in the western media, but are a cause of grave concern among U.S. and European intelligence analysts.

CHINA'S RAPID NUCLEAR ICBM ACQUISITION

"The increased closeness between the two giant states means trouble for the United States," said Ariel Cohen of the Heritage Foundation. "The Chinese will have access to the most advanced missile, thermonuclear and aerospace systems the Russians can offer."

The Soviet Union and China were bitter ideological and geopolitical adversaries for more than 30 years after a split in 1958. The first major rifts between the two powers occurred when Mao Tse-Tung and Josef Stalin vied to lead the Communist world revolution. Later, Soviet leader Nikita Khrushchev cut off nuclear cooperation with Beijing because he feared Mao would trigger a nuclear world war. Enmity culminated in 1969 when the two nations appeared to be on the brink of war over clashes in the Far East.

Only after the collapse of the Soviet Union did relations between Moscow and Beijing begin to warm. Trade across the 4,500-mile common border has expanded in recent years as emerging economic giant China hungers for Russia's wealth of raw minerals and military systems as Russia desperately seeks cash.

China's Jiang said the new Moscow-Beijing alliance "serves the basic interests of the people of both countries and is in line with international trends." Li added: "The establishment of a Sino-Russian strategic cooperative partnership...is conducive to peace and development in the Far East and in other parts of the world. On international issues, China and Russia show mutual understanding and cooperate closely in establishing a new international political and economic order that is fair and rational."

RUSSIA-CHINA ALLIANCE MAKES CHINA HIGH TECH ON LAND, SEA & AIR

As part of the agreement, China and Russia pledged to triple their annual bilateral trade to $20 billion by the year 2000. The two nations also agreed to allow China to produce Russian Sukhoi 27 fighter-bombers.

"With the money earned from the sale of Russian military equipment to China, Russia will be able to fund the development for itself of the mining pacts to build two pipelines to pump Russian oil to China, which is rapidly industrializing up-to-date types of armaments," reported Radio Russia correspondent Regina Lukashina.

THE SS-18 MISSILE, CODE NAMED "SATAN"

China has also acquired the technology and parts for Russia's most lethal intercontinental ballistic missile system, the SS-18, according to intelligence sources. This is the world's largest and most destructive ICBM. The technology transfers are being made outside official Russian channels, in an effort to avoid direct clashes with the U.S. In spite of the West's protest, the Russian-Chinese relations are at an all-time high. Recently, the two powers announced the formation of a "new strategic partnership." Russia's ICBM technology is enabling China to accurately strike targets anywhere in the United States.

The Russian defense ministry is predicting China will reduce its arsenal of intermediate-range ballistic missiles in favor of more intercontinental ballistic missiles. Currently only 14 percent of China's missiles are capable of hitting targets in the United States. The goal is to increase that percentage to around 70 percent, which the Chinese believe will give them nuclear parity with the Russians and Americans.

CHINA'S ICBM PROGRAM: FROM MEDIOCRE TO THE BEST

China is working hard to improve the accuracy of its long-range missiles and is now using sophisticated, super-accurate satellite-positioning guidance systems. "With global positioning satellite inputs, the (Chinese) large DF-15 ICBM could soon become the most accurate battlefield missile in the world," say some intelligence analysts.

China is also working on a terminal guidance system for its DF-21 intermediate-range ballistic missile. The DF-21 has a range of 1,125 miles, similar to that of the U.S. Pershing II missiles, all of which the U.S. destroyed under the 1987 Intermediate Nuclear Forces treaty with the Soviet Union.

China now maintains the largest standing army in the world. This Asian giant also has at least 17 intercontinental ballistic missiles with multiple warheads, about 70 intermediate-range ballistic missiles and 12 submarine-launched ballistic missiles. The army force includes more than 8,000 battle tanks, 1,600 light tanks and 4,500 armed personnel carriers. As the money continues to flood in, China's goal is to make her great numbers of troops much more mobile.

CHINESE GROWING NAVAL POWER SPELLS BIG TROUBLE

The Chinese navy possesses 63 submarines, 54 destroyers and frigates and 830 patrol and coastal ships. The Chinese air force has 120 medium bombers, at least 300 light bombers, 400 ground-attack fighters, 4,000 other fighters and 190 helicopters. Since 1990, Beijing has acquired 48 Su-27 Russian fighters, two Russian diesel attack submarines, 24 Mi-17 Russian assault helicopters, 10 Il-76 Russian heavy transport aircraft and as many as 100 S-300 Russian surface-to-air missiles with four mobile launchers. They have also obtained 50 T-72 Russian tanks.

Is there any reason to doubt China would use those nuclear weapons if it saw strategic value? Well, there's good reason to believe Beijing wouldn't have any moral qualms about it. Just look at the way the Chinese government treats its own people. Human Rights Watch has documented the deaths of tens of thousands of children in China's state-run orphanages where they were deliberately starved, denied medical treatment and abused by staff. As usual in China, girls face more victimization than boys. The children's bodies are routinely disposed of in crematoriums, the human-rights organization said.

CHINESE HUMAN RIGHTS WILL NOT CHANGE

"There is compelling evidence that these astonishing death rates are the result of a deliberate policy to minimize China's population of abandoned children, many of whom have been born in violation of the country's family planning regulations and are sometimes physically or mentally handicapped," said Human Rights Watch.

In addition to the mistreatment of kids, human rights activist Harry Wu charges that political prisoners are being forced to work on a major World Bank-funded agricultural project in western China. The World Bank, funded in part with U.S. taxpayer dollars, has provided loans of almost $23 billion to China. Think about it—your tax dollars are subsidizing slave labor in China!

FROM NUISANCE TO LETHAL TROUBLEMAKER

And, not coincidentally, China has some new friends in the Middle East. China is now a major supplier of arms to Iran, establishing the major link between the pre-eminent Asian power and the Middle East that students of Bible prophecy have long expected. China has sold Iran approximately $3 billion in weapons over the past several years and helped Iran to build its own missiles, helicopters and artillery, according to Western intelligence sources. But that's nothing compared to the $4.5 billion arms deal recently signed between the two countries. In addition, China has agreed to build two 300-megawatt nuclear power plants that will be operational in about seven years. The reactors, of course, could be used to build nuclear weapons.

China has also sold Iran 400 tons of chemical agents, giving it the largest chemical weapons stockpile of any undeveloped nation in the world. Such agents could be used in warheads atop Chinese-made surface-to-surface missiles that Iran has ominously placed along the Strait of Hormuz—you know, that narrow exit from the Persian Gulf through which one-fifth of the world's oil supply passes in vulnerable supertanker ships. This shipment was also reported to contain the new deadliest biological agent known to man—it has no antidote. It was created by Russian scientists who genetically engineered a strain of lethal anthrax into the most lethal agent on earth. The smallest molecule of its powdered delivery form applied to the skin brings a certain, agonizing death.

CHINA ARMS THE WORST THREATS TO THE WEST

Western intelligence agents also believe China—along with Germany and Russia—supplied the ultimate dangerous rogue, Saddam Hussein of Iraq, with the technology to develop chemical and biological weapons that threatened the allies during the Gulf War. The Chinese provided antiaircraft and air defense systems as well. Recently, China agreed to develop oil fields in southern Iraq.

Syria, likewise, buys a steady stream of Chinese arms. It seems that any enemy of the West, and particularly of the U.S., is given the most liberal of terms for any weapon in the Sino arsenal. Sensitive guidance equipment for the Chinese-made M-11 surface-to-surface missile was included in one recent shipment. Suspicions are high that Chinese equipment may be involved in an underground chemical-biological weapons factory outside Damascus. It's no secret why China is deeply involved in Middle East trade. It needs oil. China is developing faster than any other country in the world and oil is still the lifeblood of industry. Although China has vast oil reserves itself, it has been difficult to exploit them.

THE WORLD'S GREAT 'WOES' FROM THE EAST

It's with all this information in mind that we should look at this chapter of the Apocalypse. The first four trumpet judgments were mainly directed toward the earth's ecology, but the last three judgments, called "the three woes," are directed toward man himself. Each of these judgments increases in scope and magnitude as the tempo gets faster. It appears that God is putting pressure on man, a little more each time, to try to lead him to repent and turn to Jesus the Messiah for salvation. But these same judgments also harden "the religious haters of the True God" to a state of irrational thinking.

This chapter also emphasizes the war in the spiritual world that is behind all of the events that happen on earth. The activity in the realm of fallen angels, who are also called demons, greatly picks up momentum. The reality of God's restraint of evil becomes extremely apparent. The horror caused by the release of certain particularly malignant, yet awesomely powerful, fallen angels is terrifying.

Even the word "woe" which the angel pronounces on mankind should be perceived as a solemn final warning. Webster defines the word as "sorrow, calamity, affliction." If only men would heed this somber pronouncement! But the indication is that most will not.

It may seem a little confusing at first, but let me try to make clear the order of the next judgments. The first woe that is set loose on man is actually the fifth trumpet judgment (Apocalypse 9:1-12). The second woe unleashed on man is synonymous with the sixth trumpet (Apocalypse 9:13-21). The third woe is the seventh trumpet, and it includes all of the seven final, most awful catastrophes of all times, which are called the "seven judgments of the golden vials" (Apocalypse 11:14-15; 16:1-21). All of this group of "woe judgments" occur very near the end of the Tribulation period.

THE UNNATURAL *LOCUSTS* OF APOLLYON

"And the fifth angel sounded, and I saw a star fall from heaven to the earth; and the key of the bottomless pit was given to him. And he opened the bottomless pit, and smoke arose out of the pit, like the smoke of a great furnace; and the sun and the air were darkened by the smoke of the pit.

"And locusts came out of the smoke onto the earth, and power was given to them to sting like the scorpions of the earth. And they were commanded that they should not hurt the grass of the earth, nor any green thing, nor any tree, but only those men who do not have the seal of God on their foreheads. They were commanded not to kill them, but that they should be tormented five months; and their torment was like the torment of a scorpion when he strikes a man. In those days shall men seek death, and shall not find it; and shall desire to die, and death shall flee from them. The shapes of the locusts were like horses prepared for battle; and on their heads were something like crowns of gold, and their faces were like the faces of men. They had hair like the hair of women, and their teeth were like the teeth of lions. They had breastplates, that seemed to be breastplates of iron; and the sound of their wings was like the sound of chariots of many horses running to battle. They had tails like scorpions and there were stingers in their tails; and their power was to hurt men five months. They had a king over them, who is the angel of the bottomless pit, whose name in the Hebrew tongue is

Abaddon, but in the Greek tongue his name was Apollyon (The Apocalypse 9:1-11).

APOLLYON'S AIR FORCE OF HELICOPTERS

The **"star"** of Revelation 9:1 has to be a person rather than a literal star, since the personal pronoun "he" is used of it. He is also given a key and the authority to open the bottomless pit. I believe this fallen star is none other than Satan himself, described in Isaiah 14:12 as **"Lucifer"** or **"Star of the Morning."** Satan receives the key from the Lord Jesus, since He was declared the only possessor of the key to both hell and death (The Apocalypse 1:18).

HELICOPTERS DRIVEN BY THE SPIRITS OF HELL

The opening of the bottomless pit unleashes a judgment that is unparalleled in its torment of mankind. Earlier, in chapter three, I pointed out the reasons why these locusts are actually some kind of attack helicopters with a tail-mounted sprayer for chemical/biological weapons. Think about it. Open your mind to the possibilities. Don't just assume the Apocalypse is filled with unknowable symbols. Re-read the interpretation of them in chapter three. The whole principle of the Apocalypse Code indicates that John is presenting us with a first-century description of what he saw in our times! Could the punishment they inflict on man for five months be a kind of nerve gas that incapacitates man like the sting of a scorpion? Such agents already exist. In the grotesque strategy of war, leaders know that a wounded casualty is better than a dead soldier.

Why? Because it ties up several soldiers to evacuate and take care of him.

Of course, another possible interpretation is that these locusts are some sort of a demon-possessed insect. This, admittedly, is the more widely accepted view. Whatever is the case, the one who musters and drives this army is so notorious that God gives his name in both Hebrew, the original language of the Old Testament, and Greek, the original language of the New Testament. **Apollyon** in Greek and Abaddon in Hebrew both mean **"the Destroyer."** We do know from the Bible that only demons who were the most powerful, vicious, murderous, destructive and perverted in past history were locked up in the Abyss.

Apollyon appears to be the worst of them all, and second in rank only to Satan Himself. But I personally am convinced that these are literal helicopters with chemical weapons that have been gathered for this terrible purpose. Their pilots are under the direct influence of an unseen, perhaps unsuspected leader, Apollyon, the Destroyer.

There is no question what their mission is: they are used to carry out God's judgment against all mankind because of his unbelief, which He has confirmed by receiving the mark of allegiance to the Antichrist—666 plus a personal number. Those who are believers are supernaturally protected from this plague.

200 MILLION ASIANS ATTACK

"One woe is past, but now there are two more coming. Then the sixth angel sounded, and I heard a voice from the four horns of the golden altar which is before God, saying to the sixth angel who had the trumpet, 'Release the four

angels who are bound at the great river, Euphrates.' The four angels were released, who were prepared for an hour, and a day, and a month, and a year, to slay the third part of men. The number of the army of the horsemen was two hundred million: I heard the number of them.

"Now this is how I saw the horses and those who sat upon them in the vision; the riders had breastplates of fire, and of jacinth, and brimstone; and the heads of the horses were like the heads of lions, and out of their mouths issued fire and smoke and brimstone. A third of mankind was killed by these three things, by the fire, and by the smoke, and by the brimstone, which issued out of their mouths. For their power is in their mouth, and in their tails; for their tails were like serpents, and had heads, and with them they do harm" (Revelation 9:12-19).

Verse 13 begins with the second woe (the sixth trumpet). It's an especially terrifying judgment. Four of the most wicked and powerful of all fallen angels are released to inspire the destruction of a third of all remaining mankind. Remember that one-fourth of the world population has already been destroyed by the judgments described in Revelation 6:8. The poisoning of fresh-water sources killed many more. Now the remaining population is reduced by still another 33 and 1/3 percent.

DOWN BY THE RIVERSIDE

Now let me tell you about these four angels. They were bound by God because they are tremendously powerful emissaries of Satan, who control the nations of Asia with their vast population. Their confinement at the River Euphrates is especially significant. It seems that if God had not confined them, an awful war would have been started in Asia toward the Western nations long ago. But they were confined at the ancient boundary line.

The first human sin was committed in this region, in the Garden of Eden. In this area the first murder (of Abel) took place. The first great revolt against God happened (Babel). And it was in nearby Babylon that the first world ruler, named Nimrod, set up his kingdom.

The Romans, Greeks and Babylonians all considered the Euphrates River the boundary line between the East and West.

It is clear that the four fallen angels of Revelation 9:14-15 immediately mobilize this army of 200 million soldiers from the nations east of Euphrates. As I mentioned at the beginning of this chapter, Revelation chapter 16 will provide more details about this. I believe these 200 million troops will be led by the Chinese and will include other Eastern allies. It's probable that the industrial might of the Japanese will be united at this time with the economic and military might of the Chinese. For the first time in history there will be allowed a full-scale invasion of the West by the East.

THE YELLOW PERIL IS NO JOKE

Way back in 1961, the Chinese already had 200 million organized militiamen. The obvious significance of this fact is that for the first time in history there is an Asian power that can easily do exactly what this prophecy foretells. Remember that when John wrote this chapter, there were not yet 200 million people in the whole world!

It's also worth considering that there's never been such a great invasion force in history. Why not? Only

Asia could ever field such an army. As I have noted several times, it's as if God placed a boundary line there, restraining the forces that could have mobilized in Asia for a full-scale invasion. But with the releasing of these four mighty demons, there will be a full mobilization of "the kings of the East" (Revelation 16:12).

The Apostle John describes the army's mounts as horses with heads like lions and with fire, smoke and brimstone coming out of their mouths. I believe he is describing some kind of mobile ICBM launchers of the Russian SS-25 and SS-26 variety that are currently being sold to China. This great army will apparently destroy one-third of the world's remaining population while enroute from Asia to the Middle East. This could mean the destruction of the great population centers of the West. It almost certainly includes a massive nuclear ICBM strike at the United States and Europe in order to cover the movement of such a massive army.

John describes the means by which one-third of mankind will be annihilated by **"fire, smoke and brimstone."** All of these are part of a thermonuclear war: **smoke** represents the great clouds of radioactive fallout and debris, while **brimstone** is simply melted earth and building materials. China not only is a thermonuclear power now, but, as I have pointed out earlier in this chapter, also is rapidly expanding its nuclear potential.

The holocaust that ensues is again followed by an interlude. Once more, God gives man a chance to repent and turn to Jesus. Once more man refuses. The third and last woe (the seventh trumpet judgment) includes the final seven judgments which God pours out on the earth. These golden "vial" or "bowl" judgments are mercifully postponed by God until the events of Revelation 16.

It is in the intervening chapters, woven in between the chapters that carry the history forward, that many of the central characters and events of the Tribulation period are introduced and explained.

AND THEY REPENTED NOT

"And the rest of the men who were not killed by these plagues still did not repent of the works of their hands, so that they should not worship demons, and idols of gold, and silver, and bronze, and stone, and wood, which neither can see, nor hear, nor walk. Neither did they repent of their murders, nor of their sorceries, nor of their sexual immorality, nor of their thefts" (Revelation 9:20-21).

Imagine that! After everything they have seen take place on earth, men continue to turn their backs on God. These two verses also reveal that men will revert back to openly worshipping demons and idols. Not long ago, I couldn't imagine how people who have been so conditioned against the supernatural by our educational systems could do such a thing. But in recent years, we've witnessed the greatest resurgence in witchcraft, Satanism and occultism since the days of ancient Rome. Satan wants a religious world that will worship him, not atheistic rationalists.

WHEN THE OLD BLACK MAGIC STARTED A COMEBACK

Way back in 1967, about the time I began writing *The Late Great Planet Earth*, many began hailing the Age of Aquarius. But, astrologically speaking, the alignment of the planets in the shape of a pentagram just began early in 1997. This phenomenon has precipitated a surge in occult activity.

"It's a bit of a miracle that this whole thing lines up the way it does," gushes San Francisco astrologer Jim Fournier of the California Institute of Integral Studies, who has been hailing the extraterrestrial spectacle on his World Wide Web site. "You'd have to go back to 1475 to find this particular star pattern."

THE COMING "MORONIC CONVERGENCE"

To mark the occasion, New Age disciples are holding global meditations, dance parties, seances and other forms of "celebration." However, don't expect a time of "harmony and understanding," as the hit song from the musical "Hair" promised. Neither will this unusual planetary alignment usher in a period in which "sympathy and trust abound." Remember instead what the Bible says about stargazing: The sorcerers, enchanters, astrologers and monthly prognosticators will not be able to save anyone from the earth's predicted fate in the last days. They are, indeed, among the false prophets Jesus warns us about in Matthew 24:11.

But there are others—in fact, many, says God's word. And they are here. They are inside our schools, our churches and virtually every one of the world's institutions.

THE BIG-FOUR SINS

Revelation 9:21 lists the four most prominent sins of the Tribulation period. The significance of these sins is great in light of present trends in the world. It's no coincidence that the four major sins listed here are today four of the most serious problems facing law enforcement.

The first of these characteristic sins is murder. For whatever reason—societal permissiveness, lack of punishment or lack of faith—there has been an alarming increase in murder throughout the United States and the world. One factor is the rejection of absolute standards of right and wrong. When a judge who posts the Ten Commandments in his courtroom is sued, you know society has its priorities upside down.

Anyone who is awake in the latter part of the 20th century sees the violence around us. I don't think I need to elaborate on this point.

DRUGS + WITCHCRAFT = NIGHTMARE

The second prominent sin of the Tribulation era will be drug-related occultic activities. The word "sorceries" is used in Revelation 9:21. It comes from the Greek word "πηαρμακια," which means "pharmacy", and refers here to the practice of the occult tied to the use of drugs.

I didn't think I would ever see more drug use in America than I witnessed in the 1960s and early '70s. But did you know that the situation is even worse now? Drug use by teenagers has more than doubled just since 1992, with more than 11 percent now claiming to use drugs every month.

"It's an explosion of drug use," said Barry McCaffrey, director of the White House Office of National Drug Control Policy.

In recent years, President Clinton, who said he never inhaled during the '60s, has repeatedly claimed that drug use was down during his administration. Now the White House says the skyrocketing problem is part of a pattern that began before Clinton came to Washington. Either way, the situation is critical. But it's not just teen drug use that's up. Young American women are taking drugs more than ever before. According to a study by the Center on Addiction and Substance Abuse at Columbia University in New York, today's daughters are 15 times more likely than their baby-boom mothers to have begun illegal drug use by age 15.

Another category of skyrocketing use is in so-called "designer" drugs, such as methamphetamine. Hospitals across the country are besieged with drug-related episodes, according to a study by the Department of Health and Human Services.

Some say leadership in the war on drugs has been lacking—and it's not just a case of partisan politics. Liberal Democratic Rep. Charles Rangel, D-N.Y., said: "I have never, never, never seen a president who cares less about this issue."

There's a strong link between drug use and demon possession, too. As far back as 1971, the International Journal of Social Psychiatry dealt with the reality of demon possession and how to diagnose it: "There is a need to ascertain if there is any involvement in drug addiction, as it is common that addicts, especially with heroin and alcohol, become involved with black magic and vice versa. ... (Some) have been known in some cases to have been very religious people who default- ed, and thus left themselves open to some power other than God to control their lives."

THE WORSHIP OF THE CARNAL

The third prominent sin of the Tribulation will be ram- pant immorality. "Porneia," the Greek word used in this verse, refers to all kinds of sexual activity outside of marriage. Apparently, there will be a complete breakdown in the institution of marriage. Well, folks, as any-one can plainly see, we're almost there!

- More than 70,000 women are sexually assaulted every year in the United States. That's one every 45 seconds. It is the most rapidly growing violent crime in the country, the AMA said in a recent report. Three-quarters of sexual assaults are committed by a friend, acquaintance, intimate partner or family member of the victim.

- Domestic violence is more widespread than ever. Each year between 2 million and 4 million women are battered; 1,500 women are murdered by their intimate partners; 1.8 million elderly are victims of maltreatment; 1.7 million child-abuse reports are filed.

- President Clinton vetoed a bill, passed with bi-partisan support in the House and Senate, that would have prohibited partial-birth abortions. The procedure involves killing the baby by puncturing its skull, after the head has emerged from the birth canal. It seems nothing will be allowed to stand in the way of the 1.5 million abortions taking place in this country every year.

- The U.S. Supreme Court ruled as unconstitutional Colorado's Amendment 2 to the state constitution—a simple and popular attempt to prohibit local governments from turning homosexuals and other sexual deviates into the latest protected political class. By the court's reasoning, as dissenting Justice Antonin Scalia pointed out, any state that bans polygamy is also in trouble.

- It's actually a matter of debate—believe it or not—in the House of Representatives and U.S. Senate, whether men should be allowed to marry men and women marry women.

For the last 25 years, America has been engulfed in a culture war that threatens the nation's very foundation—its very survival. God's word tells us in Luke 12:48 that **"For everyone to whom much is given, from him much will be required; and to whom much has been committed, of him they will ask the more."** In the history of the world has any nation been more blessed than the United States? Yet there is always a cost to immorality. And today we are beginning to pay it.

In the last 30 years there has been a 560 percent increase in violent crime. Illegitimate births have increased 419 percent. Divorce rates have tripled. The number of children living in single-parent homes has tripled. The teen suicide rate has increased 200 percent. Student Achievement Tests have plummeted 80 points.

Have you ever wondered where the United States—the world's sole remaining superpower—fits into the end-times prophetic scenario? There are no direct references in scripture to a nation that can unequivocally and unmistakably be identified as America. How could this be? If the United States has remained the pre-eminent world power, one would expect it to be prominently mentioned in the detailed descriptions of the conflicts in the last days.

It seems a good guess that America will decline in global stature and authority before the return of our Lord and the events that lead up to that great event. We cannot rule out the possibility that the United States will be a part of the revived Roman Empire that rules over the world and breeds an evil dictator with an assignment from hell. But the Bible is clear that the real power in those final days will be seated in Europe. So, for one reason or another, America will take a back seat.

It should not surprise us. Billy Graham said years ago that if God didn't judge America soon he would have to apologize to Sodom and Gomorrah. That statement makes more sense today than perhaps ever before as the U.S. plunges even further into a moral and spiritual abyss.

But it's not just the United States. The entire world is in a headlong plunge into the morality of Sodom and Gomorrah and, unfortunately, into the same judgment.

CRIME ON THE INCREASE

The fourth characteristic of the Tribulation will be thievery of all kinds. I hardly need to convince you that this crime—in all of its manifestations—is on the upsurge today. The experts say a youth-crime crisis is right around the corner. At the current growth rate, there will be nearly a half-million more adolescent boys in the year 2010 than there are today. That trend would mean there will be 30,000 more chronic juvenile delinquents on the street in 15 years. Though representing only 7 percent of all male teens, these chronic offenders commit 70 percent of all serious crime in their age group.

"Our state and nation are awash in a tidal wave of violence, violence that has reached epidemic proportions especially among our youngest generation," said a recent report by the Washington State Department of Community Development.

Faith in the criminal justice system to punish the guilty and protect the innocent has eroded even further after the O.J. Simpson trial. One distinguished British journalist wrote after observing the jury in the case:

"The thought that one day such individuals might actually decide your fate, will, if you are innocent, fill you with absolute terror."

In America's urban centers, fear is everywhere. People are leaving their homes, their jobs and their friends to move to safer communities, but they are increasingly hard to find. It's nearly impossible to get away from the pre-teen pregnancies, the free condom distribution in public schools, the drive-by shootings, the kiddie porn, the abortion on demand, the suicide machines and the child abuse.

Since 1960 there has been a 560 percent increase in violent crime. In the last 30 years, illegitimate births have increased 419 percent. Divorce rates have tripled. The number of children living in single-parent homes has tripled. The teen suicide rate has increased 200 percent.

Again, such troubles are not limited to the United States alone. In fact, sometimes the whole world seems to be going mad, as ethnic wars, genocide and the slaughter of the innocents continues unabated on virtually every continent in the world. While everyone is talking about peace treaties in the Middle East, the president of Israel is shot down in the streets. While NATO moves a force of "peacekeeping" troops into Bosnia, the agreement between the warring groups is already planting seeds for new battles in the 800-year-old war. While the world's attention is focused on the Balkan crisis, Burundi is on the verge of wholesale ethnic slaughter between the Hutu tribe and the Tutsis. The last great attempt by the West to force peace upon a people has resulted only in fostering more violence and a new dictatorship in Haiti.

DON'T BE SHOCKED, FLEE TO THE ONLY HOPE

What goes on here? Well, it's something that should surprise no one—especially those familiar with Bible prophecy, which explains just how badly conditions on earth will deteriorate in the days just before Jesus' return.

"But realize this," Paul wrote in II Timothy 3:1-5, **"that in the last days difficult times will come. For men will be lovers of self, lovers of money, boastful, arrogant, revilers, disobedient to parents, ungrateful, unholy, unloving, irreconcilable, malicious gossips, without self-control, brutal, haters of good, treacherous, reckless, conceited, lovers of pleasure rather than lovers of God; holding to a form of godliness, although they have denied its power; and avoid such men as these."**

Maybe now the Apocalypse is beginning to sound a little less allegorical and a little more real? I hope so.

TWO COUNTERFEIT MESSIAHS

CHAPTER NINE

"And through his shrewdness he will cause
deceit to succeed by his influence;
and he will magnify
himself in his heart, and by means
of peace he will destroy many."

—Daniel 8:25

Remember Daniel's famous prophecy? Long before the Apostle John had his visions of the Apocalypse, the Hebrew prophet Daniel had a dream in which he saw four great beasts come up out of the sea. The first beast was like a lion, but had eagle's wings. The second beast was like a bear; the third beast was like a leopard, but had four heads. The fourth animal was **"dreadful and terrible"**—it had iron teeth and 10 horns. Angels explained to Daniel that the great beasts were **"four kingdoms, which shall arise out of the earth."**

The first kingdom, as I pointed out earlier, was Babylon. The second kingdom was the Media-Persian

Empire. The Greek Empire came next, just as Daniel had dreamed. Then around 68 B.C., the fourth and greatest kingdom seized world power. In phase one, this kingdom gained world authority, then it crumbled, and, just as the Scriptures have accurately predicted with its predecessors, it will rise again during this Tribulation period, or perhaps just before.

THE ROMAN ANTICHRIST

Heading up this world power will be a man of such magnetism and power that he will become the greatest dictator the world has ever known. He is the one known as the Antichrist—a seemingly messianic figure who purports to have answers to all the world's problems. He will be extremely charismatic, attractive, beguiling. He will dazzle the world with miracles produced by the very real power of Satan.

He will be a supreme humanist, however, explaining passionately how man can solve his own dilemmas. He will not accept the Bible's evaluation that man is on the verge of chaos because of sin. In fact, like many humanists we know today, he will probably react violently to the suggestion that sin is the root cause of our problems.

He will believe—and many will agree with him— that he is doing a good thing by bringing repressive measures against believers, whom he will consider "non-progressives." This Antichrist will be against every solution the Bible presents for the world's problems, and because he'll be so persuasive, he'll turn the whole world against Christ.

For years I have been telling you to keep your eyes on Europe. That's where much of the prophetic scenario remains to be fulfilled. You see, the Antichrist must come out of the old Roman culture and rise to power out of Rome because of the specific prophecy of Daniel 9:26: **"And the people of the prince who is to come shall destroy the city** [Jerusalem] **and the sanctuary** [the Temple]."

Now, in 70 A.D., the city and the Temple were destroyed by the Roman Tenth Legion. Its leader was Titus of Rome. So, clearly, the Antichrist must come from the old Roman people and culture and rule from Rome, as is reinforced in Revelation 13:

"Then I stood upon the sand of the sea, and saw a beast rise up out of the sea, having seven heads and ten horns, and upon his horns ten crowns, and upon his heads the name of blasphemy. The beast which I saw was like a leopard, and his feet were like the feet of a bear, and his mouth like the mouth of a lion; and the dragon gave him his power, and his seat [throne], and great authority.

"I saw one of his heads as though it were mortally wounded; and his mortal wound was healed, and all the world wondered after the beast. And they worshiped the dragon who gave power to the beast; and they worshiped the beast, saying, 'Who is like the beast? Who is able to make war with him?'

"There was given to him a mouth speaking great things and blasphemies, and power was given to him to continue forty and two months. And he opened his mouth in blasphemy against God, to blaspheme his name, and his tabernacle, and those who dwell in heaven. And it was given to him to make war with the saints, and to overcome them; and power was given him over all

kindreds, and tongues, and nations. And all who dwell upon the earth shall worship him, whose names are not written in the Book of Life of the Lamb slain from the foundation of the world.

"If anyone has an ear, let him hear. He who leads into captivity shall go into captivity; he who kills with the sword must be killed with the sword. In this is the patience and the faith of the saints" (Apocalypse 13:1-10).

Notice, first, that the Antichrist **"rises out of the sea."** This is a code symbol which is later defined in Chapter 17:1,15. Verse 1 talks about **"the great harlot who sits on many waters."** And verse 15 explains what those waters are: **"The waters which you saw, where the harlot sits, are peoples, multitudes, nations, and tongues."** In Biblical usage, the ocean pictures the restless strivings of the nations of the world. As Isaiah put it: **"The wicked are like the troubled sea, when it cannot rest, whose waters cast up mire and dirt"** (Isaiah 57:20). It's from this chaos of the nations that the Antichrist will rise.

HORNS, HEADS AND CROWNS

What do the ten horns represent? In the biblical symbology, horns almost always represent power. In this case, the beast's 10 horns picture 10 nations that will form the confederacy which the beast will rule during the Tribulation period.

One of the reasons I'm convinced we're living in the days just before this Tribulation period is the emergence of the European Union. There is no doubt in my mind that it is the precursor to the Revived Roman Empire to which both John and Daniel refer. Daniel also said that this confederacy would be the greatest Gentile power ever to gain control of the whole world, and he suggests that it would acquire that control through its economic strength and its leader.

Did you know that the European Union is already the world's largest economy and trading bloc? But Europe is much more than that today. In fact, it is rapidly moving toward complete legal, political and military union as well.

ONE-WORLD GOVERNMENT COMING SOON

Reflect back on the fact that way back in 1918, Russian Communist Leon Trotsky wrote in *Bolshevism and World Peace:* "The task of the proletariat is to create a United States of Europe, as the foundation for the United States of the World." That the world is also moving toward a one-world government can no longer be disputed by honest and knowledgeable men today. Think about this: Independence Hall in Philadelphia, one of the most important symbols of American freedom and sovereignty, has been placed under United Nations jurisdiction as a "World Heritage Area."

It's one of at least 17 historic sites in the U.S. now controlled—to one extent or another—by the U.N. Others include the Statue of Liberty, Yellowstone National Park, Everglades National Park, Yosemite National Park, the Grand Canyon and the Great Smoky Mountains National Park.

Independence Hall was the site of the signing of the Declaration of Independence on July 4, 1776. It was there that George Washington was appointed commander-in-chief of the Continental Army. It was there that the American flag was approved in 1777. It was there that the Articles of Confederation were ratified and the Constitution was written. Quietly, and without fanfare, the U.S. government is yielding national sovereignty and the very principles upon which the nation was founded, as "one nation under God." Clearly, as Europe advances and global government emerges, the last remaining true superpower on earth—the United States—will have to decline. As treasonous as it is, that's exactly where many of our nation's leaders are bringing us today.

By reconstructing a world government out of the ruins of the ancient Roman Empire, the Antichrist will have accomplished what no one has been able to do since A.D. 476, the year the Roman Empire officially fell. Charlemagne tried to put it back together and failed. Napoleon did his best, but the dream ended at Waterloo. Bismarck dreamed of making Germany the capital of revived Rome, and did succeed in defeating France. Hitler tried again. But his efforts resulted in the downfall of his own nation.

So fruitless were the efforts of men to reconstruct the Roman Empire that poets wrote sonnets about the futility of it all. Did you know the children's nursery rhyme "Humpty Dumpty" was originally written about the fallen Roman Empire and the attempts to put it back together?

A STRANGE-LOOKING BEAST

Notice that in Revelation 13:2, the Antichrist-beast is compared with a leopard, a bear and a lion. He will, in other words, combine the ferocity and distinguishing characteristics of the three prominent world empires which preceded him. The ancient Greek Empire struck its foes like a leopard. The Media-Persian Empire had the raw power of a powerful bear. The Babylonian Empire was famous for its regal splendor. The Revived Roman Empire will also revive the "best" of all these kingdoms.

As brilliant as he is, notice from where the Antichrist derives his power.: **"The dragon gave him his power and his seat [throne], and great authority"** (Revelation 13:2). During the last half of the Tribulation period, God will allow Satan to give the Antichrist tremendous supernatural ability. So great will be the Antichrist's influence over the world that "every tribe and people and tongue and nation" will yield to his sway. For the first time in the history of the world, Satan will get what he's been after all these years—the worldwide worship of earth's people.

He will gain this popularity either by performing a fantastic miracle or by simulating one which will fool the people into thinking it was real. In verse 3, John says that he saw one of the beast's heads as if he had been killed. When this apparently mortal head wound is somehow miraculously healed by Satan, the whole world will follow after him in amazement. You can understand that. Imagine the impact it would make on the world today if one of our national leaders appeared to be resurrected from the dead after an assassination.

On top of that, this Antichrist really will appear to improve conditions on earth. Using his super-human wisdom to overcome poverty, hunger and war, he'll *appear* to be the Messiah. And he won't be bashful about taking full credit and proclaiming himself as God. Once the Antichrist has the allegiance of the people, his true colors emerge. No more Mr. Nice Guy. No more peace and prosperity. For three and one-half years, he blasphemes God and His worshippers, ultimately killing a great many of the Tribulation saints.

LAMB'S BOOK OF LIFE

In verse 8, John speaks of a book called "the Book of Life of the Lamb." In this book are written the names of every person who ever lived on the face of the earth. When a person rejects Jesus Christ as Savior, and God is convinced he will never change his mind, that man's name is blotted out of the Book of Life. Those whose names are no longer in God's book will be the ones who will worship Antichrist.

Satan will be so angry with those whose names have not been expunged from the book that he will have the Antichrist wage a war on them. All over the world, believers will suffer and die for their faith during this period. They won't resist, but, rather, they will submit willingly, just like the thousands of martyrs before them.

THE OTHER COUNTERFEIT MESSIAH

"But, wait a minute, Hal," you might say at this time. "I know all about the Antichrist, but who's this other counterfeit messiah your chapter heading refers to?" Good question. Let's proceed through the next section of the Apocalypse to find out.

"As I looked, another beast came up out of the earth. He had two horns like a lamb, but he spoke like a dragon. He exercises all the power of the first beast before him, and causes the earth and those who dwell on it to worship the first beast, whose mortal wound was healed. He performs great wonders, so that he makes fire come down from heaven on the earth in the sight of men. He deceives those who dwell on the earth

by means of those miracles which he had power to do in the sight of the beast, saying to those who dwell on the earth, that they should make an image to the beast, who had the wound by the sword, and yet lived. He has power to give life to the image of the beast, so that the image of the beast can both speak, and cause as many as will not worship the image of the beast to be killed. He will cause all, small and great, rich and poor, free and enslaved, to receive a mark in their right hand, or in their foreheads.

"And no man can buy or sell unless he has the mark, or the name of the beast, or the number of his name. Here is wisdom. Let the one who has understanding count the number of the beast; for it is the number of a man; and his number is six hundred and sixty-six" (Revelation 13:11-18).

So what we have here is a two-for-one deal. If you liked the first beast, you'll love the second. He is a co-conspirator in this one-world endgame. He's even more ruthless than the first beast because he will enslave men's minds and souls. He will have the same kind of scintillating personality, the same tireless dynamism, the same oratorical finesse. He will also have the same Satanic powers.

But notice the differences. Whereas the first beast emerged from the sea (the unrest of troubled nations), the second beast emerges from the land. When the Bible uses the word **"land"** symbolically, it usually refers to the land of Israel.

"Well," you might say, "it looks to me like the verse says '**earth**,' not '**land**.' " But let's get back to the original Greek. The term τησ γησ, when used in a context involving Israel, is assumed to mean **"the Land of Israel"** unless otherwise clearly noted.

This interpretation of the False Prophet being an Israeli also makes sense because Jews would never accept a Gentile as their Messiah. This second beast will be the Messiah to the Jews, just as the Antichrist will be the False Messiah to the Gentiles and later claims to be God himself. You see how Satan has the whole deceitful plan laid out?

A RELIGIOUS BEAST

Like the first beast, the second one wears horns. However, the second one has only two uncrowned horns (not ten crowned ones, as the first Antichrist). What kind of power do these two horns symbolize? Not political, but religious. That's why he is known as "the False Prophet." He will successfully amalgamate all religious systems into one counterfeit one. His two horns are like those of a lamb, which indicates he will seek to imitate the false idea about the Messiah the Jews hold to.

Millions will fall for this deception, and when the religious merger is complete, Satan will have accomplished one of the most fiendish plots of all time—a blasphemous imitation of the triune God. Think about it. The first beast will masquerade as the Messiah. The liberated demons (Revelation 16:13-14) will imitate the power of the Holy Spirit. Is it any wonder why so many will be fooled?

Here are seven things the False Prophet will do:

1. He exercises unlimited authority (Rev. 13:12).
2. He forces people to worship the Antichrist (verse 12).

3. He performs great miracles (verse 13).
4. He deceives the population (verse 14).
5. He forces people to worship the Antichrist's image in the Temple (verse 14).
6. He murders all nonconformists (verse 15).
7. He forces people to receive **"the mark of the beast"** (verse 16).

THE GREAT PRETENDER

What kind of "great miracles" does the False Prophet perform? An example is given in verse 13. Through Satanic power he makes fire streak from the sky to the earth in the sight of astonished onlookers. Through this and other spectacular miracles the False Prophet will convince most people that he is the God-sent Messiah. Satan knows all too well what kind of showmanship will impress the curious crowds. Remember, he persuaded one-third of all the angels in heaven to follow him. Imagine how easy it is for him to dazzle man.

That's why we need to be on guard even before the Tribulation period. Have you noticed how much supernatural hocus-pocus is going on around us today? Remember: Not all miracles are from God. The increase in demonic miracles is just another sign of the times.

THE MARK OF THE BEAST

In verse 15, the False Prophet gives life to the image of the first beast, the Roman Antichrist. Then he forces people to worship the image under the penalty of death. Where do you suppose the image will be erected? Right in the Holy of Holies of the reconstructed Temple.

The term **"abomination of** [that causes]

desolation" is a technical Jewish term for the desecration of the Holy of Holies. This happened once before in 165 BC, when Antiochus Epiphanes entered the Holy of Holies of the Second Temple, set up an image of a pagan god and sacrificed a pig before it. The "Abomination" referred to by Jesus as preceding His Second Coming is the one Daniel predicted as **"the abomination of desolation"** in Daniel 9:27 and 12:11.

The False Prophet will perfect a way to expose everyone who believes in Jesus Christ. All beast-worshippers will receive a distinguishing mark on their right hand or their forehead. Everyone who refuses the mark will be cut off from economic survival. They will be forbidden to buy or sell anything. Now, how could that have happened in the first century? The answer is, "it couldn't." Before the advent of computer technology and other high-tech gimmickry, it would have been impossible for the government to number all people on earth, let alone enforce whether they buy or sell without a valid number. Of course, today this is an easy task for modern computers.

THE HIGH PRICE OF THE NUMBER

What will happen to the millions of people who succumb to the False Prophet's threats and receive the beast's number? The Apostle John gives us the answer: **"If any man worships the beast and his image, and receives his mark in his forehead, or in his hand, the same shall drink of the wine of the wrath of God, which is poured out without mixture into the cup of His indignation; and he shall be tormented with fire and brimstone in the** presence of the holy angels, and in the presence of the Lamb" (Revelation 14:9-10).

And what is the meaning of this number? Down through the years, lots of Bible scholars have tried to figure out exactly what it's all about. But I don't think it's a big mystery. Since the number 6 in the Bible stands for man, I believe the meaning of 666 is man trying to imitate the trinity of God (three sixes in one person). Therefore, anyone who acknowledges this blasphemous trinity by worshipping the 666 beast will be separated forever from the one true triune God.

THE SHOCKING CAREER OF A BEAUTIFUL WHORE

CHAPTER TEN

"And the woman was clothed in purple and scarlet, and adorned with gold and precious stones and pearls, having a gold cup full of abominations and of the unclean things of her immorality. ...And the woman whom you saw is the great city [Rome], which is reigning over the kings of the earth."

—Revelation 17:4, 18

In Revelation 17 and 18 the Apostle John deviates, once again, from the chronological story of future history to provide a flashback to the development of the two great dynamics behind the meteoric rise of the Revived Roman Empire to world domination. Many of the esoteric symbols used in the Book of Daniel and previously in the Apocalypse are explained in these passages.

Be warned that there are some "complex encoded concepts" put forward here. Some of the principal personalities symbolize two different yet similar ideas. To make the most of the material, I suggest reading it all first.

THE WHORE
AND HER PARAMOURS

"Then there came one of the seven angels who had the seven bowls, and talked with me, saying to me, 'Come here; I will show to you the judgment of the great whore who sits upon many waters; with whom the kings of the earth have committed fornication, and the inhabitants of the earth have made drunk with the wine of her fornication.'

"So he carried me away in the Spirit into the wilderness and I saw a woman sitting upon a scarlet-colored beast, full of names of blasphemy, having seven heads and ten horns. The woman was clothed in purple and scarlet color, and lavished with gold and precious stones and pearls, having a golden cup in her hand, full of abominations and filthiness of her fornication;

"Upon her forehead was a name written, MYSTERY, BABYLON THE GREAT, THE MOTHER OF WHORES AND ABOMINATIONS OF THE EARTH.

"I saw the woman drunk with the blood of the saints, and with the blood of the martyrs of Jesus; and when I saw her, I wondered in amazement.

"And the angel said to me, 'Why are you so amazed? I will tell you the mystery of the woman, and of the beast that carries her, which has the seven heads and ten horns.

"'The beast that you saw was, and is not, and shall ascend out of the bottomless pit, and go into perdition; and they who dwell on the earth, whose names were not written in the Book of

Life from the foundation of the world, shall wonder when they behold the beast that was, and is not, yet is.

"'Here is the mind which has wisdom. The seven heads are seven mountains, on which the woman sits. And they are seven kingdoms: five are fallen, and one is, and the other is not yet come; and when it comes, it must continue a short while. And the beast that was, and is not, is himself the eighth, and yet is out of the seventh: and he will lead into perdition.

"'And the ten horns which you saw are ten kings, who have received no kingdom as yet, but receive power as kings one hour with the beast. These have one mind, and shall give their power and authority to the beast. These shall make war with the Lamb, but the Lamb shall overcome them; for He is Lord of Lords, and King of Kings, and those who are with Him are called, and chosen, and faithful.'

"And he said to me, 'The waters which you saw, where the harlot sits, are peoples, and multitudes, and nations, and tongues. The ten horns which you saw upon the beast, these shall hate the harlot, and shall make her desolate and naked, and shall eat her flesh, and burn her with fire. For God has put in their hearts to fulfill His will, and to agree, and give their kingdom to the beast, until the words of God have been fulfilled.

"'And the woman whom you saw is that great city, which reigns over the kings of the earth'" (Revelation 17:1-18).

WHO'S WHO IN PROPHECY

Now what is all this about? To grasp the colossal concepts explained and predicted in this chapter, it is important to crack the code. Many mysterious symbols used in both Daniel and Revelation are clarified. Let's begin with the two central figures—a whore and a weird, seven-headed, ten-horned beast.

THE GREAT WHORE

Have you ever noticed the way some things that are evil are both fascinating and repugnant at the same time? My sister-in-law, Johanna Michaelson, once wrote a book called *The Beautiful Side of Evil.* And, indeed, there is a beautiful side to evil. After all, the father of evil, Satan, was once Lucifer, the most beautiful and perfect creature God ever made.

Likewise, when the Apostle John was shown the vision of the great Harlot, he was both spellbound and repulsed. He couldn't take his eyes off this woman who was the epitome of evil. She was lavishly decked out in jewels and luxurious garments of royalty. The cup she held out in her hand was of rich gold on the outside, but inside it was filled with putrefying things. She looked like she had just come from a Halloween party, for she had a bizarre name garishly written on her forehead: "Babylon the Great, Mother of Harlots and the Abomination of the Earth." The most disgusting and horrible thing about her was that she was drunk—but it wasn't alcohol that got her that way. It was blood— the blood of believers!

When John gets his first glimpse of this Harlot, she's sitting on this weird creature—a monster just as repulsive as the whore. It has seven heads and ten horns. Blasphemous names are written all over it. It is scarlet, the color of blood. Sounds like a fitting companion for the whore.

WHAT'S IT ALL ABOUT, JOHN?

As John stands there scratching his head and wondering what this nightmare is all about, the angel begins to unravel the mystifying sight. He begins by exposing just how gross this whore really is. All the kings of the earth have committed adultery with her, and she is so immoral that she has intoxicated the majority of people on the earth. When she is said to "sit on many waters," it means she has control over vast numbers of people whom she has seduced in some way (verse 15).

A SHORT HISTORY OF UNHAPPY HOOKERS

What's the worst name a woman can be called? Let's face it. For most women, being called a "whore" is about as low as you can get. So, for the angel to label this particular woman with that name must have great significance.

How can the kings of the earth commit adultery with her and all the people become drunk with her immorality? In the Bible, the terms **"whore," "harlot"** and **"adulterer"** are frequently used to symbolize a spiritual departure from God and His truth by an individual, a city or a nation. The word "harlot" is especially used to describe a religion that is counterfeit. Isaiah the Prophet lamented over Jerusalem, **"How is the faithful city** [Jerusalem] **become a harlot...?"** (Isaiah 1:21). Jeremiah rebuked the nation of Israel for indulging in the demonic religions of her neighbors:

"You [Israel] **have lain down as a harlot"** (see Jeremiah chapter 3). Ezekiel also chastised Israel with God's words: **"I signed a covenant with you, and you became mine. ...You took the very jewels and gold and silver ornaments I gave to you and made statues of men and worshiped them, which is adultery against Me"** (Ezekiel 16:8, 17, TLB).

The word "harlot" was also connected with the practice of witchcraft when the prophet Nahum pronounced judgment upon the great ancient city of Nineveh: **"Because of the multitude of the harlotries of the charming harlot, the mistress of witchcrafts, that sells nations through her harlotries, and families through her witchcrafts"** (Nahum 3:4). Isaiah also called the city of Tyre a harlot.

In the Tribulation period, it won't be a city or a nation that is practicing this spiritual adultery. It will be the entire world, or "world-system," as James called it. The world-system is the organized system of world attitudes and institutions that excludes God's way and is under Satan's control. We can see the beginnings of this system in our own world today.

When a nation, founded as one nation under God, gives up its sovereignty under God in favor of "interdependence" on the world, you can see where the future lies. To be a friend of this future system in the sense of compromising God's viewpoint of life and letting the world squeeze you into its mold is to commit adultery, spiritually speaking.

Remember, also, that in a true relationship with God through Jesus Christ, believers are viewed as being the "Bride" of Christ (II Corinthians 11:2). That's another reason that playing around with false religion is viewed throughout the Bible as spiritual adultery.

THAT OLD INTOXICATING SPELL

In all the references we just looked at in Israel's history of seductions, each time she was lured away from her Jehovah God it was by a perversion of religion. And so it is with the great Harlot which John sees. She symbolizes an enormous false religious system that is so appealing that she has been able to seduce all the kings of the earth with her deceptions. Not only will this seductive religious prostitute wield control over the leaders of the nations, but even the common man will be intoxicated with her.

What kind of religious system can we expect under the Harlot? What powerful secrets will she hold that permit her to bring together atheists, Buddhists, Muslims, Hindus and cultural (but unbelieving) Christians? Most interpreters of this chapter have simply updated the thinking of the Protestant reformers who believed that the Pope would be the Antichrist and the Roman Catholic Church the whore of Babylon. In my opinion, this is inaccurate—a little to simple. The Catholic Church has been steadily declining in popularity and it's difficult to imagine any Pope—even one as popular as John Paul II—being able to rein in Muslims under his leadership.

The main question is this: How could any false brand of Christianity get all the other religions to join it? The religious system of the Tribulation period will, in my opinion, have to offer more than some watered-down brand of false Christianity to muster an appeal on the broad scale described here. Many churches today have already learned through their declining attendance that watered-down Christianity bores people to death.

BABYLON THE GREAT

The answer to this dilemma is unveiled in the "mystery" of the whore's name on her forehead—"Babylon the Great, the Mother of Whores and the Abominations of the Earth." This great Harlot is associated with an ancient city that immediately brings to mind sinful, lustful, depraved religion and life—Babylon!

What is it about Babylon of old that this great false religion will emulate? A cardinal rule for interpreting symbols in the Bible is to examine their first biblical usage and every successive occurrence. When we do this carefully with the concept of Babylon, the meaning is both clear and startling.

THE BIRTH OF BABYLON

The historical drama of Babylon began on the plains of Shinar, where the first world dictator established the world's first religious center. The dictator's name was Nimrod, which means "We will revolt." He's described literally as "a mighty hunter of men in defiance of the Lord."

The beginning of this kingdom was Babel, or Babylon (Genesis 10:8-10). Under this leader, the first united religious act was performed—the building of a tower "whose top would reach into the heavens" (Genesis 11:4).

These people were smart enough to know that they couldn't build a tower through which they could climb up to where God lives. That wasn't of interest to them at all. You see, they were already studying the stars and the moon and were codifying the first system of astrology. The tower was to aid them in better observation of the stars. It was, in essence, an astrological observatory. Many centuries later, when

God pronounced future judgment on Babylon, He said that **"she had labored with . sorceries and astrology from her youth,"** indicating that these were practiced in Babylon from her very beginning in history (Isaiah 47:12–13).

DANIEL IN BABYLON'S DEN

In the seventh century BC, the Prophet Daniel, while captive in Babylon, was made a member of the king's special advisors.These men were all steeped in the religion of Babylon, which had now reached a very sophisticated stage.When the king had a nightmare one night, he called for his advisors to interpret what it meant. **"Then the king commanded to summon the magicians, the astrologers** [conjurers, incantationists], **the sorcerers, and the Chaldeans, to reveal to the king his dreams..."** (Daniel 2:2).

Who were these people? The magicians practiced black magic and performed various supernatural feats through contact with demon spirits. The conjurers were specialists at seances and at making objects miraculously materialize. By calling on the spirits of the dead, they made contact with demons, who then impersonated the dead person being summoned. The sorcerer specialized in witchcraft. The Chaldean was the highest of all the advisors. He was part of a special priestly caste perpetuated by inheritance, a race that could trace its family history back to the originators of astrology. So a Chaldean was a master astrologer.

BABYLON AND THE HARLOT

When the angel told John that he would tell him the mystery of the woman, he meant that this Harlot, the false religious system, would have as its main teachings the same occultic practices as ancient Babylon. It would include black magic, demon contact, seances, miraculous materializations, witchcraft, astrology and sorcery. Her luxurious external appearance of jewels and royal clothes meant that she would have a great appeal to the sensual nature of men, but her gold cup filled with abominations represented her corrupt and perverse teachings. Her drunkenness with the saints' blood showed how she had successfully eliminated all who opposed her.

Just as Wall Street is synonymous with the whole investment world and as Madison Avenue brings to mind slick advertising, so the name Babylon symbolizes occultism in every form.

FROM EMPIRE TO EMPIRE

We know that the ancient city of Babylon was ruled by this occultic influence, but not many people are aware that the religion of Babylon passed from empire to empire until the days of ancient Rome. The mystery that John was seeking to unveil for his readers was that religious Babylon would be revived to control the last great world power in the last days of history. This religion will be an occultic amalgamation of all the world's religions. For the first three-and-a-half years of the Tribulation, it will enjoy a position of great power and influence over the Revived Roman Empire and its leader, the Antichrist.

With all that in mind, let's analyze the riddle of the beast with seven heads and ten horns (the monster upon which the whore sits). Verses 9 and 10 of Revelation chapter 17 tell us that the seven heads represent two things: seven mountains and seven kingdoms (literally). I believe the seven mountains refer to the seven hills of the city of Rome. Rome has been associated with her seven hills throughout Roman literature and on coins of her day. What's being said here is that the Babylonish religious system was controlling the Rome of John's day, and indeed was synonymous with Rome itself. Rome was the center of pagan worship.

However, John tells us that the seven heads also represent seven kingdoms; five have fallen, one is, and the other is still to come. Here he is referring to those great world empires from the time of the original Babylon of Nimrod's day which have been dominated by the false occultic religion of Babylon.

The first kingdom was Assyria, with its occult-mad capital city of Nineveh (see Nahum 3:4). The second was Egypt, which devoted much of its total wealth to the construction of the pyramids, all built according to astrological specifications. Egypt was also given to black magic (see Exodus 7:11, 22; 8:7, 18; II Timothy 3:9). The third was the neo-Babylonian empire of Daniel's day, which really perfected the black arts. The fourth was Medo-Persia, which conquered Babylon but was in turn enslaved by the Babylonian religion. The fifth was the Greek empire. One visit to Greece and her ancient temple sites will convince you of the sway which idolatrous religions held there.

Running through the culture of all these great past empires was an underlying belief in astrology. This was the cohesive force that bound together all the witchcraft, sorcery and magic. Kings would seldom make a move without consulting advisors steeped in the ancient art of Babylonian religion. The ancient priests enjoyed royal stature and power, especially in Egypt.

When John speaks of the "five kingdoms that have

fallen," he means the five I just mentioned. But then he says, "One is." This has to refer to the great empire of his day, Rome, which was filled with the same occultic beliefs that had originated on the plains of Shinar in ancient Babylon. This was the sixth kingdom of John's vision.

John looks to the future when he says of the seventh head (kingdom), **"...the other is not yet come; and when it comes, it must continue a short while"** (Revelation 17:10c). This refers to the future revival of the Roman empire.

This seventh head is different from the other six because it has ten horns on it. This indicates that this seventh kingdom will be made up of ten nations from the old Roman Empire (the sixth head), which will have confederated. In my opinion, this unquestionably refers to the European Union, which I believe is destined to bloom into the last great world empire, represented by the seventh head with the ten horns. This Revived Roman Empire will become dominated by the same Babylonish religious system that has ridden herd on the past great world empires.

A CLOSER LOOK AT THE BEAST

After having given John a panoramic view of all the past world powers and their seduction by the Harlot of Babylon, the angel now narrows his focus to the "beast" in its final form. Looking from this perspective, he says the beast was and is not, and then will exist again and be destroyed. He must be referring to the fact that Rome existed in his day, but that a day was coming when it would no longer exist. Then it would rise again and be destroyed.

As you review the history of Rome, you recall that

it was never conquered by anyone; it fell from within because of its own decadence. For nearly 15 centuries, Rome has not existed as a viable world political power. But the move in Europe today is destined to put the old Roman Empire back together again.

Thus the Revived Roman Empire is referred to as a beast, as is the scintillating world leader who will control it and is also known as the Roman Antichrist. Although the "beast" we are looking at in this chapter has only seven heads, John says that it briefly sprouts another, an eighth head, but this head is really an outgrowth of the seventh (the Revived Roman Empire) and is quickly destroyed. I think of it as a wart that grows out of the seventh head and is cut off.

THE WART

This "wart" speaks of both the Antichrist himself and his kingdom, which will emerge full-blown during the last half of the Tribulation. It will be an extension of the Revived Roman Empire. When the Antichrist becomes indwelt with Satan at the middle of the Tribulation, his kingdom from that point on will take a different tone. The whole world will worship the beast instead of the Harlot. He will rule with force and deception, but the people will be completely spellbound by his clairvoyant abilities. Apparently they'll be mesmerized to the point where they won't even realize how repressive the government has become.

On the basis of John's prophecy of the rise of Babylon the Great and on the basis of the latest evidence of current events, I believe the stage is very nearly set for the resurrection of this great, occultic religious system. Eastern culture has always been open to various forms of the occult, but now the West is also experiencing a great fascination with the black arts and dark religions.

This truth really threw me for a jolt when I saw how prevalent the occult is in the lives of our children—our future leaders. But it's not just the kids. A whole generation which grew up in the 1960s seems to have been brainwashed with an anti-biblical worldview. Now even the Christian churches are being targeted for conversion by pagans.

A group called the Temple of Understanding, affiliated with the Gaia Institute and the United Nations Global Committee of Parliamentarians on Population Development, is behind a new push to inundate Christian churches with nature-worshipping propaganda. The effort is organized under the auspices of the National Religious Partnership for the Environment, which works with the U.S. Catholic Conference, the National Council of Churches, the Coalition on the Environment and Jewish Life and the Evangelical Environmental Network. The $5 million program, funded by Ted Turner and other liberal foundations, attempts to politicize 100 million Americans in 53,000 congregations.

"It is unmistakably clear that the new partnership is the brain child of anti-Christian New Age pagans who promote an environmental religion known as Gaia," says Tom DeWeese, president of the American Policy Center.

The partnership has sent to 53,000 congregations, including every Catholic parish and every Jewish synagogue in the nation, "education and action kits." The kits contain Sunday school and sermon resource material carefully planned to fit into the doctrine of the particular denomination targeted.

A pillar of the Temple of Understanding is a man named Maurice Strong, who was secretary-general of the first U.N. Earth Summit, which called for 50 percent of the land in each of the 50 states to be turned into wilderness areas where no humans would be allowed to enter. Strong, a millionaire proponent of one-world government, owns a ranch in Colorado where he has built a Babylonian sun god temple which serves as the center of New Age religious activities.

The whole world was shocked in March 1997 by the story of the W. W. Higher Source cult when 39 Southern California members apparently committed suicide as part of their belief that they would leave their bodies and hook up with an alien spaceship trailing the Hale-Bopp comet. Someone once said that when people stop believing in God they start believing in anything. If ever there were a better illustration of that truism than the Higher Source cult, I can't think of what it is.

Even witchcraft, once a source of jokes in western culture, is getting new respectability in this New Age. Recently, witches have won a court fight to use a non-denominational New Hampshire cathedral as a meeting place. The state human rights commission ruled that since the non-profit foundation that supervises the cathedral allowed a variety of religious groups to use the facility, it could not discriminate against witches.

What goes on here? The answer is we are entering an age in which the ancient Babylonian religion will once again move front and center and reunify the whole world.

THE BEGINNING OF THE END

Do you remember how Chapter 16 of the Apocalypse closed? All the cities of the world were destroyed, and a great war was about to trigger the personal appearance of Jesus Christ back to this earth to restore it to its original beauty. This climactic event, which we call "the Second Coming of Jesus Christ," is described in detail in Chapter 19.

Between Chapter 16 and 19, we are given a parenthetical description of the destruction of two cities, each called Babylon. One is a religious system and the other is an economic colossus. As we saw in Revelation 17, the religious system was not really a city at all in the sense of having a specific geographical location. It was instead a religious influence which had attracted itself to many cities during its long and blasphemous history since the days of its origin in ancient Babylon.

The question that comes to mind is, "When the Antichrist destroys this Harlot in the middle of the Tribulation, does he destroy some geographical location from which she rules?" I personally don't think so, since that would mean destroying his own kingdom. I believe it is more likely that he will purge the leaders of the false religious system, confiscate all of its wealth and proclaim himself God.

In Revelation 18, however, we see an entirely different picture. This Babylon is indeed a specific location. It's the center of commerce, trade and industry in the last half of the Tribulation. It will be so vital to the economic and cultural life of the whole world that when it is destroyed in one hour's time the whole world will be plunged into mourning.

WILL BABYLON BE REBUILT?

Where will this great commercial Babylon be located? There are many reputable Bible scholars who believe that this Babylon is going to be an actual rebuilt city at the ancient site of the destroyed city on the Euphrates River. One of the reasons for their belief is Isaiah's prophecy about the ultimate destruction of Babylon. He said it would be destroyed by the Lord Almighty when the day of the Lord was near (Isaiah 13:1, 6-7,19-20). "The day of the Lord" refers to the period which immediately surrounds the coming of Christ. Since the city of Babylon has not existed historically since the days of Alexander the Great, it would have to be rebuilt to be destroyed.

Another line of reasoning that seems to point to the rebuilding of Babylon is a prophecy by Zechariah about the last days. He speaks about a temple being built in the land of Shinar, which is Babylon (Zechariah 5:5-11). Well, with all that in mind, it probably won't surprise you to know that Saddam Hussein has been spending a fortune rebuilding Babylon in modern-day Iraq.

But let's not be dogmatic about this. While I believe Babylon will be rebuilt, other Bible students believe with equal conviction that the Babylon being discussed here is a secular system of commerce and culture alienated from God. They believe it could be a great city in America, Europe or Asia.

WHY REBUILD BABYLON?

If Babylon is actually to be rebuilt, what would be the purpose and function of the city? Would it be the economic giant we see in this chapter? I don't think so. It's hard to imagine how any city located in the hostile Arab world could rise to such world prominence with all the kings of the earth free to go in and out and conduct their business. That's why I believe Babylon will be rebuilt, not as the commercial and economic enter of the world, but as the center of the "harlot" religious system for a short while.

Zechariah affirms this reason for its rebuilding and the means by which it will be rebuilt with these words: **"The angel who talked with me went forth, and said, 'Lift up your eyes now, and see what this is that is going forth.' And I said, 'What is it?' And he said, 'This is an ephah that is going forth.' Again he said, 'This is their appearance throughout the land.' As I beheld, there was lifted up a talent of lead; and there sitting in the midst of the ephah was a woman. And he said to me, 'This is wickedness!' And he cast her down into the middle of the ephah; then he cast the weight of lead over its opening.**

"Then I lifted up my eyes and looked, and two women were coming out with the wind in their wings; for they had wings like the wings of a stork, and they lifted up the ephah off the earth into the sky.

"Then I said to the angel who talked with me, 'Where are they taking the ephah?' And he said to me, 'To build for her a temple in the land of Shinar [Babylon]**; and she will be established there upon her own base'"** (Zechariah 5:5-11).

THE EPHAH

An ephah was a symbol of commerce in Zechariah's day. It was a unit of dry measure which symbolized commercial and economic affairs. In fact, the symbol of two winged women holding an ephah and a balanced scale has for centuries been the recognized symbol of commerce. You can still find medallions with this picture on it, and many chambers of commerce still use this symbol.

Here in this prophecy the ephah represents the whole Satanic world system, including all the godless commercialism and hedonistic worship of luxury and pleasure which economic success permits. Zechariah also introduces a woman, who is at first seen sitting comfortably in the middle of this ephah (the godless commercial system). Here she is in intimate contact with all the worldly wealth and commerce by which she is supported and in which she delights.

But then Zechariah tells us that the angel pronounced an indictment of wickedness on the woman and threw her down into the middle of the ephah, restraining her there by means of a lead covering.

WHAT HAPPENS
TO THE WOMAN?

How can this woman sit contentedly in the middle of this economic and commercial system (the ephah) and yet want to escape from it so badly that she has to be restrained? I'll get to that in a minute, but let's first see what happens to this woman. She is picked up while still in the ephah and transported by two sympathetic women companions to the land of Shinar, the site of ancient Babylon. There the ephah was to build a temple for the woman and to establish her in it.

Let me unscramble this prophecy for you. I believe the woman Zechariah speaks of is the religious Babylonish system which we saw in Revelation 17. It had its roots in the dark religion of ancient occultic Babylon. The ephah in which this woman settles refers prophetically to the Revived Roman Empire and Rome. For awhile, this ecclesiastical Harlot is content to dwell in Rome. But some time before the middle of the Tribulation she begins to get the idea that she isn't too popular with the Antichrist and his kingdom anymore, so she seeks to move her base and decides on Babylon. This is where all the magic, sorcery and astrology began, after all.

Using the wealth she had accumulated by her stay within the "ephah" of Rome, she flees to Babylon with the support of the Antichrist. Shortly afterward, however, the Roman Antichrist regrets he let such wealth and power slip out of his grasp. Realizing he no longer needs the Harlot, he destroys her. It's possible he destroys Babylon at the same time. But I tend to think God reserves that privilege for himself at the end of the Tribulation.

For the next three-and-a-half years the Antichrist reigns as God on earth, killing the saints and coercing men to worship him. Then his great capital city, which I believe is Rome, is destroyed by the true God of heaven. This is the subject of Revelation 18.

Now is a good time for you to read all 24 verses of chapter 18, keeping in mind that the chapter is describing the destruction of the most influential city in all of history (with the exception of Jerusalem). This "Babylon" must be located near a large body of water, since the smoke of its burning is seen by all kinds of ship personnel. It's also a great center of commerce, culture and luxury and has a history of persecuting God's saints.

I believe this city can only be Rome. It's

inconceivable to me that the Antichrist could be the most powerful ruler of the world, controlling a kingdom which surpasses all previous world empires in wealth and power, without having as his capital city the great economic center described in this chapter. How could Rome not be the capital of the Revived Roman Empire? That this great city is called "Babylon" is no surprise either. It's synonymous with all the evil, corruption, dissoluteness, sensuality and perversion of ancient Babylon and its reprobate child, religion.

"After these things I saw another angel come down from heaven, having great authority, and the earth was made bright with his glory. He cried mightily with a strong voice, saying, 'Babylon the Great is fallen, is fallen, and has become the habitation of demons, and of every foul spirit, and a cage of every unclean and hateful bird. For all nations have drunk of the wine of the wrath of her fornication, and the kings of the earth have committed fornication with her, and the merchants of the earth have grown rich through the power of her luxuries.'

"I heard another voice from heaven, saying, 'Come out of her, my people, in order that you may not be partakers of her sins, and that you do not receive her plagues; for her sins have reached to heaven, and God has remembered her iniquities. Reward her even as she rewarded you, and pay her back double according to her works; in the cup of torture which she filled for others, fill to her double. As much as she has glorified herself, and lived luxuriously, so much torment and sorrow give her, for she said in her heart, "I sit as a queen, and am no widow, and shall never

see sorrow." Therefore shall her plagues come in one day, death, and mourning, and famine, and she shall be utterly burned with fire; for strong is the Lord God who judges her.

"'The merchants of the earth shall weep and mourn over her; for no man buys their merchandise any more; the merchandise of gold and silver and precious stones, and pearls, and fine linen, and purple, and silk, and scarlet, and every kind of citron wood, and all kinds of vessels of ivory, and all kinds of vessels of precious wood, and of bronze, and iron, and marble, and cinnamon, and incense and perfumes, and ointments, and frankincense, and wine, and oil, and fine flour, and wheat, and cattle, and sheep, and horses, and chariots, and slaves, and souls of men.

"'And the fruits that your soul so desired have departed from you, and all things which were luxurious and sumptuous have departed from you, and you will not find them anymore. The merchants of these things, who were made rich by her, shall stand a distance away because of the fear of her torment, weeping and wailing, and saying, "Woe, woe, the great city that was clothed in fine linen, and purple, and scarlet, and adorned with gold, and precious stones, and pearls! For in one hour such great wealth has been destroyed."

"'And every shipmaster, and all the ship companies, and sailors, and as many as trade by the sea, stood a distance away, and cried when they saw the smoke of her burning, saying, "What city is like this great city?" They cast dust on their heads, and cried, weeping and wailing, saying,

"Woe, woe, the great city, in which all who had ships on the seas were made rich by reason of her wealth! For in one hour she has been destroyed." Rejoice over her, you who dwell in heaven, and you holy apostles and prophets; for God has avenged you on her.'

"And a mighty angel took up a stone like a great millstone, and cast it into the sea, saying, 'In this same violent way that great city, Babylon, will be thrown down, and will not be found again. And the music of harpers, and minstrels, and flute players, and trumpeters will not be heard anymore in you; and no craftsman, and whatever craft he may be, will be found anymore in you; and the light of a lamp will not shine anymore in you; and the voice of the bridegroom and the bride will not be heard anymore in you; for your merchants were the great men of the earth; for by your sorceries all nations were deceived. And in her was found the blood of the prophets, and of saints, and of all that were slain upon the earth'" (Revelation 18:1-24).

Notice who it is that weeps over the fall of Babylon, the great city which is Rome. It's the merchants—the businessmen. It's very possible that this will be the capital of the world at this time. That's why it's the center of banking, finance, trade, culture, government, agriculture, industry and the arts. The panic that follows will be 100 times greater than that which followed the stock market crash of 1929.

Notice also that this superpower will deal not only with commodities, but also with the souls of men (verse 13). How this is possible is revealed in verse 23: **"For your merchants were the great men of the**

earth; for by your sorceries all the nations were deceived." Evidently through the religious system, the Antichrist, and the False Prophet, men will be drawn under the hypnotic power of demons through sorcery and will actually sell their souls to Satan in exchange for this favor. Because no one will be able to buy or sell without the mark of the beast, this will give him total control over every facet of the lives of those who have sworn allegiance to him.

This strikingly attractive man whom the Bible calls the beast, with seemingly so much care and concern for all the peoples' needs and with brilliant solutions to some of the world's toughest problems—all presented with such mesmerizing charm—will turn out to be the greatest curse the world has ever known. Those without a knowledge of the Bible will be swept along with him into destruction.

SEVEN VIALS OF EARTH'S DESTRUCTION

CHAPTER ELEVEN

**"...And the kings of the whole inhabited earth were gathered together for the WAR of the Great Day of The ALMIGHTY GOD.
...And the wine press was trodden outside the city [Jerusalem], and blood came out of the wine press, up to the horses' bridles,
for a distance of two hundred miles."**

—The Apocalypse 16:14b; 14:20

Toward the end of the Tribulation period, God reluctantly closes the gates of heaven. He decides that the unbelievers left on earth have hardened their hearts to the gospel and will never turn to Him. Then He prepares to pour out the seven climactic "golden vials" on the earth. These contain the final judgments of God on those who refused to accept His offer of a free pardon purchased at the awful cost of the death of His beloved Son. They are sent forth by the direct mighty command of God booming out of the special burning incense pouring out of the heavenly Temple. The fragrant incense smoke that always burned in the Temple was a symbol of the believers' prayers coming before God for over 3000 years.

"Then I heard a great voice out of the Temple saying to the seven angels, 'Go your ways, and pour out the bowls of the wrath of God upon the earth'" (Apocalypse 16:1).

The seven angels who administer this solemn work are dressed in the uniform of priests—white robes and golden vests. Since it was as priests that they had presented the prayers of the martyred saints before God, it's fitting that they should carry the bowls (actually golden censers used in the Temple for carrying incense, the symbol of prayers) of retributive judgment in answer to those prayers.

"And the first went, and poured out his bowl upon the earth, and there fell a malignant, painful sore upon the men who had the mark of the beast, and upon those who worshiped his image" (Apocalypse 16:2).

As previously reported, even though we live in the age of "miracle drugs", today there are many diseases for which we have no cure. In fact, as I mentioned earlier, some of our most effective medicines and antibiotics are no longer working. Many doctors are expressing concern that the indiscriminate use of antibiotics has made the germs immune to them. Thus, we see new epidemics—from AIDS to Gulf War syndrome—in which people simply cannot resist infection.

There is also growing concern over the development of "superbacteria" which can't be stopped by any of the drugs the medical community currently maintains in its arsenal. Several strains of the flu virus have fallen into this category. Bubonic plague has made a remarkable resurgence in recent years. In some remote locations, even the old Biblical plague of leprosy has increased at alarming rates.

But what's the most dreaded disease of our time? AIDS, perhaps, but far more people fear cancer because of its prevalence. Nothing strikes terror in a person's heart in the latter part of the 20th century like the words, "I'm sorry, the biopsy showed malignancy." However, the malady the first angel pours out onto the earth will produce such intense suffering that cancer would seem like a welcome relief by comparison. There will be no cure for this malignancy, and it will afflict all unbelievers who have sworn allegiance to the Antichrist. The miraculous protective power of God will be at work in the believers of the Tribulation, otherwise not one would survive to re-populate the new earth and the kingdom of the Messiah.

Now, this rash of sores could easily be caused by the tremendous radioactive pollution in the atmosphere. After the bombings of Nagasaki and Hiroshima, thousands of people developed hideous sores because of the radioactivity. But notice that this malady affects people selectively. God supernaturally protects the believers from this horrible plague, as He did when a similar condition was inflicted on Egypt in the days of Moses (Exodus 9:8-11).

THE DAY THE OCEANS DIE

"The second angel poured out his bowl upon the sea, and it became like the blood of a dead man; and every living soul that was in the sea died" (Apocalypse 16:3).

Another judgment follows rapidly on the heels of the terrible plague. The second angel poured his bowl on the sea, and it became blood like that of a dead man. Every living thing in the sea died. Everything!

Throughout the Apocalypse, God has been taking drastic, yet carefully measured steps of judgment against the world. But think of the consequences of destroying all life in the sea! Think of how many people depend on food from the ocean to live. And this is not to mention the tragedy of millions of life forms becoming extinct in a day. This will be Greenpeace's worst nightmare.

This is a maximum-judgment destruction of the oceans—just like the skin cancers of the last one.

"Well, Hal," you might ask, "Isn't God being kind of cruel to bring such terrible judgments on the world?" One of the reasons the Apocalypse describes the terrible things which God will allow is to shake us up in hopes man will see the need for God right now. The judgments all through the Apocalypse have increased in a measured progression; but, finally, after man still refuses to turn to God, all the stops are pulled out. Mankind tends to think that God's long-suffering is weakness.

The reason I say the judgments are carefully measured is because the same kind of judgments take place in a less intense form earlier in the Apocalypse. For example, the judgments of Apocalypse chapter 8 are similar to those of Apocalypse chapter 16, except the former are less frequent and less severe. In Apocalypse chapter 8, verses 8 and 9, only a third of the sea became blood and only a third of the marine life died. But in Revelation 16, ALL marine life is wiped out.

We can only speculate as to whether a direct

judgment of God, a final insane launch of all remaining nuclear weapons, or perhaps some as yet unknown weapon of man will be used to destroy marine life to this extent. But this we do know—there is enough nuclear firepower in the current arsenals of the very nations predicted as combatants in this final great war to do everything predicted in this 16th chapter of the Apocalypse.

ALL FRESH WATER POLLUTED

"The third angel poured out his bowl upon the rivers and fountains of waters, and they became blood. I heard the angel of the waters say, 'You are righteous, O Lord, who are, and was, and shall be, because You have judged in this way. For they have shed the blood of saints and prophets, and You have given them blood to drink; for they deserve it.' I heard another out of the altar say, 'Even so, LORD God Almighty, true and righteous are Your judgments'" (Revelation 16:4-7).

As if the bloodied sea weren't enough, the third angel will pour out his bowl of judgment into the rivers and springs of waters, and they also will become blood. It gets extremely grim when there is no fresh water to drink anywhere on earth. There's going to be a big run on Coca-Cola®, Pepsi®, and bottled drinks of every kind. But you know that won't last longer than a few weeks at most.

In verse 6 we're told why God inflicts this horrible judgment on the earth: **"They have shed the blood of saints and prophets, and You have given them blood to drink. They deserve it."**

As we've seen already, the most vicious and bloody time of persecution of believers is going to take place during this seven-year Tribulation period. The slaughter will be performed, not by irreligious men, but by religious men—men who are part of a great one-world reli-. gious institution.

HATRED IN THE AGE OF TOLERANCE

There's nothing more vindictive than a religious person who has rejected the truth of the Bible and wants to get rid of a few contenders. Religion has always been very hard on its competition. There's never been much tolerance for someone who says that Jesus Christ is the only way to God. Many people are proud of their "open-mindedness and tolerance." But their open mind instantly becomes very narrow, defensive and uptight when someone quotes Jesus as saying, **"I am the Way, the Truth, and the Life. No one comes to God except through Me"** (John 14:6). During the Tribulation, people will be ready, willing and able to spill the blood of Christ's believers and the slaughter will be instigated by apostate religion.

The horror will get worse toward the end of the Tribulation. The followers of the Antichrist will pour out the blood of the saints, and God in turn will give them blood to drink.

AND NOW—THE GLOBAL HEAT WAVE FROM HELL

"And the fourth angel poured out his bowl upon the sun, and power was given to him to scorch men with fire. And men were scorched with

great heat, and blasphemed the name of God, who has power over these plagues; and they did not repent so as to give Him glory" (Revelation 16:8-9)

What happens in the aftermath of a full-scale nuclear war? We've already discussed some of the environmental crises that would ensue. But one of the overlooked effects would be the burning of nitrogen in the upper atmosphere. The nitrogen would be converted to oxides of nitrogen, which would then combine with and destroy what's left of the protective ozone layer in the earth's stratosphere. Damage to that layer, as we have seen in recent years, can have serious consequences for the biology of the planet. Destruction of the ozone layer, which could result from an all-out nuclear war, would be disastrous for all life on the planet.

So, imagine the scene: As the clouds from the nuclear holocaust begin to dissipate, holes in the ozone layer let in deadly radiation, heating up the planet's surface until it becomes unbearably hot. This will be one of the worst judgments that man will experience, since there will be no fresh water to drink to gain relief—and, given the state of the planet at this time, I doubt if there will be air-conditioning in working order. In fact, electricity will be virtually knocked out.

But look, even after this brutal judgment, mankind will still refuse to repent. One of the reasons I don't believe in purgatory—or some middle ground between heaven and hell—is this: When men reject Jesus Christ, even a foretaste of hell doesn't make them change their minds.

CLOUDS OF DEATH OVER ROME

"And the fifth angel poured out his bowl upon the throne of the beast, and his kingdom was full of darkness; and they gnawed their tongues for pain, and blasphemed the God of heaven because of their pains and their sores, and still did not repent of their deeds" (Apocalypse 16:10-11).

What's John talking about when he refers to the judgment falling upon the throne of the beast and his kingdom? He is talking about the Revived Roman Empire, which the beast will lead, and its capital, none other than "The Eternal City"—Rome. In the interpretation of Apocalypse chapter 17, this will be documented through the Apocalypse Code.

Notice also that tremendous darkness envelops the beast's kingdom. This same phenomenon occurred in Egypt during the plagues; the whole land was consumed in darkness so oppressive that Moses said you could actually feel it. I think that's the sort of thing that will come upon the kingdom of the Antichrist at this time. Remember, it will be the religious center of the world. This divine judgment will give a physical illustration of their spiritual darkness.

Why will it get so dark? It could for the purpose of allowing the final deployment of the 200 million Asian soldiers into the area of the Middle East. This is the next judgment.

ASIA'S MARCH TO ARMAGEDDON

"The sixth angel poured out his bowl upon the great river, Euphrates, and its water was dried up, in order that the way of the kings of the East

might be prepared. And I saw three unclean spirits, like frogs, come out of the mouth of the dragon, and out of the mouth of the beast, and out of the mouth of the False Prophet. For they are the spirits of demons, working miracles, going forth to the kings of the earth and of the WHOLE WORLD, to gather them to the battle of that great day of God Almighty. ('Behold, I am coming as a thief. Blessed is he who watches, and keeps his garments, lest he walk naked, and they see his shame.') And he gathered them together into a place called in the Hebrew tongue Armageddon" (Apocalypse 16:12-16).

The sixth bowl of judgment is a horrifying extension of the judgment of the sixth trumpet recorded in Chapter 9. You'll recall that the sixth trumpet revealed the vast hordes of Asia mustered to prepare to march into the Middle East under cover of what appeared to be a limited nuclear strike. In this present situation of the sixth bowl, the terrifying army of 200 million Asians has reached the banks of the Euphrates, the ancient boundary between the East and the West.

But how will this great army cross the mighty Euphrates? Did you know that it would not have been possible for even a much smaller invading force to cross until the 1990s? That's right. Only recently has Turkey completed work on a dam project that literally allows that nation to turn off the headwaters to the Euphrates at any time. In fact, in tests already conducted, Turkey has at times reduced the mighty Euphrates to a mere trickle—causing tensions between Ankara, Turkey's capital, and Damascus, which relies so heavily on the flow of water.

THE WEST MOBILIZES FOR WAR

Keep in mind, again, that Satan (referred to as "the dragon"), the Roman Antichrist and the False Prophet will be the unholy and false trinity of this Tribulation period. John describes demon spirits that proceed first from the mouth of Satan and then from the two world leaders. These three personalities act virtually as one, setting into action demons who perform miraculous signs in front of the leaders of the world. Since the Eastern leaders are massed at the Euphrates in preparation for an invasion, these miraculous signs must be performed mostly for the benefit of those world leaders from the West. Why? Because the unholy trinity is trying to mobilize forces to fight against this Asian invasion, who have already been mobilized and motivated by the four mighty angels who were released from their long-term imprisonment at the Euprates. I believe that there will be a great display of demon-produced miracles that will dazzle and mesmerize these nations into converging on Israel and squaring off against the kings of the East.

WORLD WAR III

The first stage of this war begins with a coordinated attack of the Arab-African Confederacy (called **"the king of the south"** in Daniel 11:40) launching a massive attack on Israel. The second phase of this is the immediate, almost simultaneous, full-scale invasion against Israel by Russia and its allies (**"the king of the north"**). The first stage of the War of Armageddon commences with the opening of the **Second Seal** (Apocalypse 6:3-4) when the red apocalyptic horseman goes forth and takes peace from the earth. The

Russians will sweep down to take command of their Muslim allies, and continue right through Israel into Egypt and Africa. It appears that the Muslims may be double-crossed by Russia. The Russian commander's takeover of Egypt at this time is puzzling. Perhaps Egypt refused to join this confederacy because of its dominance by Iran and radical fundamentalist Islam.

While the Russian commander is in Egypt preparing to attack and consolidate the African continent under his control, **"rumors from the East and the North will disturb him..."** (Daniel 11:44). As the commander looks east from Egypt, his intelligence sources warn him of the Asian army's massive movement of its troops westward toward Syria and Israel. As the Russian leader checks north, his sources inform him that the Rome-led E.U. is preparing a mighty counterattack, most likely to cut off his supply lines. The Roman Antichrist will rush to Israel's defense after the attack, since the False-Prophet-led Israel has signed a defense pact with the Antichrist which commits him to protect Israel (Daniel 9:27).

The second stage of the war begins when the Russians quickly return from Egypt to regroup their forces in Israel and make sure their supply lines are not cut off. Their command post will be set up in Jerusalem, ironically on the Temple Mount (Daniel 11:44b, 45).

THE TERRIBLE END OF MAGOG AND HIS CONFEDERACY

The third stage of the campaign finds the Russian army and its Muslim allies completely annihilated in Israel and its environs by the European forces of the Roman Antichrist (Daniel 11:45b; Ezekiel 38:18-39:5).

HOW THE APOCALYPSE CODE WAS SET UP

Ezekiel adds a further eyewitness description of this horrific future battle between Russia and allies and the Revived Roman force in his prediction of **"a torrential rain of hailstones, fire and brimstone"** (Ezekiel 38:22). I've mentioned before some of the anticipated consequences of an unrestricted nuclear war. These are some of the phenomena that neither Ezekiel nor John could have understood as time travelers to the beginning of the third millennium AD. But today, scientists furnish information that makes these phenomena understandable. From past experiences with hydrogen bomb tests, we know that the enormous blast compresses and pushes humidity instantly into the upper stratosphere. The humidity, compressed into a large quantity of water, is quickly frozen into huge chunks. These giant hailstones fall back to earth in chunks of over 100 pounds. This answers why the prophets reported seeing *"ice, fire and molten earth"* in the holocausts they witnessed. Today, it's data like these that form the Apocalypse code which unseals and deciphers prophecies previously unknowable.

Part of the consequences of this confrontation will be the devastation of the homelands of Russia and her satellite forces. Israel will also suffer greatly from this unprecedented warfare, but miraculously, it will not be destroyed. Ezekiel 39:5-8 predicts that the fire of these weapons will also fall upon many of the great population centers of the world, described as **"those who inhabit the coastlands in safety."** "Coastlands" is an apocalyptic code word for the great Gentile civilizations as Ezekiel knew them. Today, the Hebrew word for coastlands could be interpreted **"continents"** of the Gentiles.

HISTORY'S FIRST FULL-SCALE INVASION OF THE WEST BY THE EAST

The fourth stage of the war is when the 200-million-man army from the Asian Confederacy, led by China, reaches the Euphrates and prepares to attack the Antichrist's forces now occupying Israel. In Apocalypse chapter 9, John revealed that the Divine restraint of the vast populations of Asia attacking the West was removed. Not only was it taken away, but one of the horns of the golden altar of incense orders the release of the four mighty fallen angels that were bound at the ancient east/west boundary formed by the Euphrates River. I say "fallen angels" because the angels of God are never bound.

Other important details in the judgment of the sixth trumpet are *the horn* and *the golden altar* which are in the presence of God. Now in the typology of this part of the Divinely designed Tabernacle/Temple, the **golden altar of continuously offered incense** was symbolic of the believers' prayers constantly floating up to God. The **horns of the altar** were symbolic of its power. So it is the power of the prayers of, in this case the Tribulation believers, that causes the release of this judgment upon apparently those most responsible for the slaughter of the innocent believers in Jesus as Messiah and Savior.

These fallen angels apparently are extremely vicious and have great powers of deception. In the scheme of Satan's world system, they must have supreme authority over Asia. It is especially chilling to review the prediction about them: **"Release the four angels who are bound at the great river**

Euphrates. And the four angels, who [had prepared themselves] **for the HOUR and DAY and MONTH and YEAR, were released, so that they might kill a third of mankind. And the number of the armies of the cavalry was TWO HUNDRED MILLION: I heard the number of them"** (Apocalypse 9:14-16).

The fifth stage is the mobilization of the rest of the world's remaining armies to fight under the command of the Antichrist against **"the kings of the East."** At this point, all the armies move into the Middle East and spread out along the entire length and breadth of Israel, with the greatest concentration poised for the fiercest and final battles fought on the Plains of Armageddon and the enviorons of Jerusalem, which is part of the war of Armageddon (Apocalypse 16:13,14 and 14:20).

THE FINAL HOLOCAUST

It's almost impossible for us to imagine the magnitude of what is predicted here. Just imagine—at least 300 million soldiers strung out across the entire Middle East and poised for the final mad act in man's most finely developed art—war. The human waves of the East are pitted against the superior weaponry and technology of the West. The horrible carnage of the war is beyond our comprehension. John says, **"the blood will stand to the horses' bridles for 200 miles in the Jordan Valley"** (Apocalypse 14:20).

THE DESTRUCTION OF ALL CITIES

"The seventh angel poured out his bowl into the air, and there came a great voice out of the

Temple of heaven, from the throne, saying, 'It is done.' And there were voices, and thunders, and lightnings; and there was a great earthquake, such as was not since men were upon the earth, so mighty an earthquake, and so great. And the great city was divided into three parts, and the cities of the nations fell; and great Babylon came in remembrance before God, to give to her the cup of the wine of the fierceness of His wrath. And every island fled away, and the mountains were not found. And there fell upon men a great hail out of heaven, every stone weighing about one hundred pounds, and men blasphemed God because of the plague of the hail; for the plague was exceedingly great" (Revelation 16:17-21).

While this great battle is raging, every city in the world is going to be leveled. This will take place by what is called an "earthquake" (σεισμος, the Greek word here, simply means a violent shaking, not necessarily by an earthquake). But that's not the only meaning. The word itself simply means "a great shaking of the earth." The earth could be shaken by a literal earthquake or by a full-scale nuclear exchange of all remaining missiles. I lean toward the nuclear conflict, but, of course, the nuclear could well trigger the other. But notice that, at the same time, "the cities of the nations fall." New York, London, Paris, Berlin, Tokyo, etc.—*all* will be destroyed at this time.

WHAT ABOUT THE U.S.?

Many people have wondered what the United States will be doing during this conflict. We've already seen that the U.S. is destined to lose its role as the leader of the West as the Roman leader emerges. There's no scriptural indication that the U.S. will be wiped out before this time, so we can only deduce that she will be a part of this western confederacy which unifies against the great Asian power. However, in this last outpouring of judgment, no nation will escape—every city in the world will be leveled.

WHOLESALE SLAUGHTER

This chapter closes with multiplied millions of soldiers slaughtering each other in and around Israel. In the process, the cities of the world will have been reduced to rubble. Is all this enough to convince the survivors that the Christian martyrs were right? Oh, no. Look at what they do instead: **"Men blasphemed God because of the plague of hail...."** (Revelation 16:21).

Is this the end of the world? Hardly. In fact, as we'll soon see, it really marks a new beginning. It's the beginning of a wonderful New World Order that will never be destroyed. Stay tuned—it gets better!

Zechariah 14:12 predicts the plague that will destroy the soldiers who attacked Jerusalem. He predicts that **"their flesh will be consumed from their bones, their eyes burned out of their sockets, and their tongues consumed out of their mouths while they stand upon their feet."**

THE SECOND COMING OF JESUS THE MESSIAH

CHAPTER TWELVE

"For then there will be great Tribulation,
such as has not been from the beginning of the
world until now, no, and never will be.
And if those days were not shortened,
no human being would be left alive..."

—Matthew 24:21,22b

A hhh, but those days will be shortened. God is merciful. Not everyone will perish. In fact, the very reason God subjects humanity to the judgments of the Apocalypse is because He wishes that no one should perish. But mankind has not been paying attention. The world needs a wake-up call.

For sheer drama, it would be difficult to find any literature to compare with Revelation 19. Consider the stark contrasts it offers:

There are two suppers—one of sublime purity and joy as the Lamb takes His beloved bride, and the other of utter repugnance and horror, as vultures come to devour the mountains of human bodies killed in the last mad battle on earth.

There are two responses to Jesus Christ—one a spontaneous thunder of praise about the rightness of God's judgments, and the other a hail of blasphemy and bullets to resist the King's return to His earth.

There are two rewards—one a dazzling robe of white linen given to each believer as he enters heaven, and the other a blinding flash of the naked power of Jesus Christ as He reduces to a sea of blood all those who wave their fists in defiance with their last ounce of strength.

WHAT TIME IS IT?

This chapter resumes the chronological timetable of the future and begins where it left off at the end of Apocalypse Chapter 16. In that chapter we saw the final acts of a godless world coming to a roaring crescendo: millions of troops deployed along a battle line from Turkey to the Arabian and Sinai Peninsula are attacking each other with an insane frenzy. Cities are leveled, hundred-pound hailstones pulverize the earth, and the planet itself reels under the force of the greatest earthquake or violent shaking from nuclear blasts in the history of mankind.

The earth will seem to be on the precipice of self-annihilation, but in heaven it will be the beginning of the end for all human suffering.

"And after these things I heard a great voice of many people in heaven, saying, 'Praise the Lord! Salvation, and glory, and honor, and power, belong to the Lord, our God; for true and righteous are His judgments; for He has judged the great Harlot, who corrupted the earth with

her fornication, and has avenged the blood of His servants at her hand.' And again they said, 'Praise the Lord!' And her smoke rose up forever and ever. And the twenty-four Elders and the four Living Beings fell down and worshiped God that sat on the throne, saying, 'Praise our God, all you His servants, and you that fear Him, both small and great.' And I heard something like the voice of a great multitude, and like the voice of many waters, and like the voice of mighty peals of thunder, saying, 'Praise the Lord! For the Lord our almighty God reigns'" (Apocalypse 19:1-6).

This glimpse at the heavenly preparation for Jesus' return to earth reveals the most spirited Jesus Rally of all time. The scene revolves around five thunderous, resounding shouts of "Praise the Lord!" (the meaning of "hallelujah") sung in unison by angels, Old Testament saints, Tribulation saints and Church-age saints.

What a contrast with the scene John paints in Revelation 9:20–21 and 16:21, where men blaspheme and curse God for the judgments befalling them. In the eyes of the unbeliever, God is never fair in what He does. When men suffer the just consequences of their actions in flaunting God's grace, rejecting His love and despising His law, they always blame God and call Him unjust.

In heaven, though, they're praising the triune God for His completed salvation promise, for His glory and power and especially for His righteous judgment on the false religious system of the great whore. With the 24 Elders and four Living Beings on their faces before God's throne and the heavenly choir joining in the five great "Praise the Lords," all creation gratefully extols the virtues of Christ their Creator.

All these beings are rejoicing at Christ's going to take His rightful reign over the earth. You see, Christ purchased the title deed to the earth on the Cross. But He hasn't yet exercised His right to the rulership of the earth. He'll do that when He comes back.

Here the saints in heaven break into the great "Hallelujah Chorus" of the Bible as Christ rises and prepares to return to the earth as King of Kings and Lord of Lords. They sing about how qualified Christ is to judge the world. Since He died for everyone, He has the right to judge those who turn down the love gift He offers them.

"'Let us be glad and rejoice, and give honor to Him; for the time of the marriage of the Lamb has come, and His bride has made herself ready.' And it was granted to her to be clothed with fine linen, clean and white; for the fine linen is the righteous acts of the saints. And he said to me, 'Write, Blessed are they who are called to the marriage supper of the Lamb.' And he said to me, 'These are the true words of God.' And I fell at his feet to worship him. And he said to me, 'Don't do that! I am your fellow servant, and one of your brothers who declares the testimony about Jesus. Worship God; for the testimony about Jesus is the spirit of prophecy' " (Revelation 19:7-10).

As I have mentioned before, the Church is the bride of Jesus Christ. All of the true believers in Jesus are considered His bride. Nothing is more descriptive of the mystery of the Church than the Apostle Paul's sublime comparison of Christian marriage with the marriage of Church-age believers to the Lord.

Ephesians 5:25-32 reveals that each person who

believes in Christ becomes a member of His body, of His flesh and bones. Then Paul writes, **"For this cause a man shall leave his father and mother and be joined to his wife, and the two shall become one flesh. This mystery is a profound one, but I am speaking about Christ and the Church."**

To better understand this marriage relationship with Christ, we need to examine the customs of the ancient world, to which Paul wrote these words. Usually three steps were involved from the initial approach to the marriage union:

- First, a marriage contract was negotiated between the parents, usually when the children were still too young to assume responsibility. This contract was a binding agreement: it meant that the two parties were legally married even though they would have no sexual contact with each other for perhaps years. This condition was known as "betrothal," but it was a much stronger tie than our present-day engagement period. It gave the two betrothed parties a chance to grow in their relationship before the actual consummation of their marriage vows.

- Second, when the couple had reached a suitable age of maturity, the groom, accompanied by his friends, would go to the home of the bride and escort her to the house which he had prepared for both of them to live in. There might be an exchange of gifts.

- Last would come the consummating event, the wedding feast. Many guests would be invited to share the celebration of this union of happy bride and groom.

Likewise, when a person—man or woman—

accepts the forgiveness provided in Jesus' death on the Cross, he or she enters into a legal contract of union with Jesus. The Holy Spirit gives new life to the man's dead human spirit, and a beautiful, growing relationship develops between Christ and the new believer. This growth is called maturing in your faith.

When Jesus returns, He is the Bridegroom coming to take His beloved bride to the home he has been preparing. There they joyously consummate their marriage vows, and the two who were previously declared one are now one in actual experience. The bride eagerly lays her dowry at Jesus' feet—that dowry of crowns which she has won for faithfulness during her betrothal period on earth. Then the Bridegroom, Jesus, gives her the rewards of a well-pleased Groom.

And who are the friends who attend the ceremony and reception? I believe they will include the Old Testament saints and the Tribulation saints who have died before the end of the Tribulation.

THE MARRIAGE SUPPER

The final step in the marriage of Christ to the Church is the wedding feast. While Revelation 19:9 pronounces a blessing on the guests at this supper, it doesn't indicate the time or place of it. One clue about where the supper will be held is Jesus' statement in Matthew 26:29 as He drinks the cup of wine at the Last Supper. He said He would not drink wine again until the day He drank it with His disciples in His Father's Kingdom.

His "Father's Kingdom" is a thousand-year reign of Christ on earth following the Tribulation period and the War of Armageddon. Remember in the Lord's Prayer, we say: **"Thy Kingdom come, Thy will be** done, on earth as it is in heaven..." (Mathew 6:10). This passage is a reference to the Millennial kingdom. It's my feeling that the wedding feast of the Lamb and His bride will take place on earth at the very beginning of the Millennial Kingdom of God.

For the next thousand years, the wedding guests join the bride and Groom in fellowship with one another on an earth that's been restored to its original beauty. This is one wedding where everybody goes home with the bride and Groom and they all live happily ever after. But more on that Millennial Kingdom in the next chapter.

A NEW WARDROBE FOR THE BRIDE

One of the most exciting parts about a wedding for the bride is deciding what the wedding gown will be like. It's customary for the bride to wear white, symbolizing that she is pure. The Apostle Paul reminds us that Christ has given us His word as a means of continual cleansing, so that He might bring us to Himself as a holy bride, without any spot or wrinkle or blemish (Ephesians 5:27).

Meanwhile, in Revelation 19, John tells us that the Lamb's bride has been given a wedding garment that would be the envy of every Paris designer. Think about it. The unlimited imagination and skill of the Great Designer of the universe have gone into the making of these gowns. They are to be made of fine linen, and this linen symbolizes the righteous deeds done by the saints while they lived on earth.

I think the point being made here is that everyone who is part of the bride—or Church—will have a linen wedding gown. But the amount of yardage in the gown will be determined by how many deeds that person performed in dependence upon the Holy Spirit's power while on earth. Isn't that an awesome thought? We need to remember that we're preparing our "garments" for eternity right now.

JOHN'S FAUX PAS

Notice what happened to John when he witnessed the breathtaking wedding scene. He was so awestruck by—and thankful for—what the angel had showed him that he fell down at the angel's feet and began worshipping him. Now, keep in mind, this was no ordinary, run-of-the-mill angel. He's described in Apocalypse 18:1 as having great authority and illuminating the earth with his glory. Yet, look what he told John about worshipping him: **"Don't do that! I am your fellow servant, and one of your brothers who declares the testimony about Jesus. Worship God: for the testimony about Jesus is the spirit of prophecy"** (Apocalypse 19:10).

That's one of my favorite passages in the whole Bible. I love the prophetic word and I feel grateful to the Lord that He has allowed me to help bring it—in popular form—to millions of people around the world. I've sat by the hour reading letters from people who have committed their lives to Christ through this message of Christ's imminent return. It's also one of the strongest motivations to believers to get their priorities in life straightened out and to mean business for the Lord in their Christian lives.

BEHOLD, A WHITE HORSE!

"And I saw heaven thrown open, and a white horse charged forth; and He who sat on it was

called Faithful and True, and in righteousness He judges and makes war. His eyes were like a flame of fire, and on His head were many crowns; and He had a name written upon Him, which no man understood, but He Himself. And He was clothed with a uniform dipped in blood; and His name was called the Word of God. And the armies that were in heaven followed Him upon white horses, clothed in fine linen, white and clean. And out of His mouth goes a sharp sword, so that with it he might strike the nations, and He shall rule them with a rod of iron; and He treads the winepress of the fierce wrath of Almighty God. And He has on His uniform and on His thigh a name written, KING OF KINGS, AND LORD OF LORDS" (Apocalypse 19:11-16).

Is Jesus really going to come back to earth? Is He really going to rule over the planet for a thousand years? Is John's description a literal one, or is this mere symbolism?

In Acts 1:8 Christ spoke His final words to His disciples before He physically left this earth. This is how Luke describes the events surrounding Christ's ascension: "And, when He had spoken these things, while they looked on, He was taken up, and a cloud received Him out of their sight. And while they were looking intently into the sky as He went up, behold, two men in white robes stood beside them" (Acts 1:9-10).

Here's the scene. Christ had just given His disciples their final briefing. He started rising up into the air and disappeared into the sky. And there they all stood gaping. The disciples had just asked Jesus if He would give the kingdom to Israel at this time. He said no, there would be an interim program before the kingdom would be established.

The disciples stood there, startled by the fact that Jesus had gone in this very sensational way. While they stood there dumfounded, two angels appeared to them in the form of men, clothed in dazzling white garments. Verses 11 and 12 continue: "**'You men of Galilee, why are you standing looking into the sky? This same Jesus, who was taken up from you into the sky, will return in exactly the same manner as you saw Him go into heaven.' Then they returned to Jerusalem from the mount called Olivet, which is near Jerusalem, a Sabbath day's journey away.**"

When Jesus physically left the earth that day, angels immediately promised that He would come back in the same way He left. And how did He leave? Bodily, physically and visibly. This wasn't symbolism the disciples witnessed that day. This was the real resurrected Jesus ascending into heaven. And He's going to come back the same way to the same place.

Zechariah goes on to tell us that the Mount of Olives will be split in two by an incredible earthquake the moment Christ's foot touches it. Did you know a geological fault has been discovered there—a faultline that runs in exactly the direction this prophecy indicates?

THE LION OF JUDAH

What other surprises does this chapter hold for us? The description of Jesus here in Revelation 19 reveals Him as a fierce warrior executing judgment upon those who have rejected Him and His offer of redemption.

What a contrast between this role and Christ's role at the First Coming, when, as the Lamb of God, He came to take away the sins of the world.

Jesus dramatically charges forth from heaven on a white stallion. A white horse has always been a symbol of conquest, as I mentioned earlier. The hands that hold the reins of this horse still bear the great scars of His crucifixion, a silent reminder to everyone being judged that He died for their sins.

A NAME ABOVE ALL NAMES

Jesus wears the many crowns of His royal and divine titles. These indicate that He's supreme in all things. He has a name written on Him that's so glorious, so much a part of His infinite character that no man can understand it.

All the clothing of King Jesus is stained in the blood of His enemies. This fulfills a prediction which the Prophet Isaiah received after he asked the Lord about a vision he had seen: **"Who is this who comes from Edom, with garments of crimson from Bozrah? ...Why is your apparel red, and your garments like one who treads in the winepress?"**

The Lord answers Isaiah, **"I have trodden the winepress alone, and of the people there was none with Me; for I will tread them in My anger, and trample them in My fury; and their blood shall be sprinkled upon My garments, and I will stain all My raiment. For the day of vengeance is in My heart, and the year of My redeemed is come"** (Isaiah 63:1-4).

THE WORD OF GOD IN FLESH

In Revelation 19:13, John tells us that Jesus' name is still "The Word of God." A few years later, when this same John wrote the Gospel which bears his name, he explained fully what it meant for Jesus to be called "The Word."

Just as my words reveal my invisible self to you, so Christ is the visible expression of the invisible God. God clothed all His thoughts toward man in the Person of Jesus. In that sense, Jesus is the ultimate communication of God to man. He's called "The Living Word" because in His person Jesus embodies everything God has to say to man. Jesus brought out this ministry, **"Have I been so long with you, and yet you have not come to know Me, Philip? He who has seen Me has seen the Father ..."** (John 14:9).

THE KING AND HIS ARMY RIDE FORTH

What a sight this great army and its Leader will make! The King's clothes are stained with red and His troops are uniformed in pure white. The soldiers are all of the redeemed in heaven, and as they follow behind their Leader they appear as a great cloud in the heavens. With a sword coming out of His mouth, He'll destroy all of His enemies and deliver the Tribulation believers who are still alive.

THE SUPPER OF FOOLS

"And I saw an angel standing in the sun, and he cried with a loud voice, saying to all the fowls that fly in the atmosphere: 'Come and gather yourselves together to the supper of the great God,

that you may eat the flesh of kings, and the flesh of captains, and the flesh of mighty men, and the flesh of horses and of those who sit on them, and the flesh of all men, both free and enslaved, both small and great.' And I saw the beast, and the kings of the earth, and their armies, gathered together to make war against Him who sat on the horse, and against His army. And the beast was seized, along with the False Prophet who performed miracles before him, with which he deceived those who had received the mark of the beast, and those who worshiped his image. These were both cast alive into the Lake of Fire burning with brimstone. And the rest of the beast's followers were slain with the sword of Him who sat upon the horse, whose sword proceeded out of His mouth; and all the fowls were filled with their flesh" (Revelation 19:17-21).

You can imagine that the hardness of men's hearts reaches its zenith at the sight of Christ's return. The forces of the Antichrist and False Prophet and the great Asian army apparently forget their animosity toward each other and unite to fight the Lord and His army. Somebody forgot to tell them that you can't fight God—and win.

Both the False Prophet who mesmerized unbelievers with his sorcery and miracles from Satan and the Roman Antichrist (beast) are now judged immediately by the Lord and cast into the Lake of Fire—while they are still conscious. Yes, I guess God does approve of capital punishment. Immediately after disposing of those two, Christ turns to judge all those still alive on earth who have rejected Him. This judgment is described in Matthew 25:31-46.

THE SHEEP AND THE GOATS

Jesus told us in Matthew 25 that when He came the second time as Judge of the World, He would separate the surviving believers symbolized by the **sheep** from the unbelievers symbolized by the **goats**. The **sheep** would be those people who had evidenced their faith in Him by the way they treated a group He called **"these brothers of mine."** As I mentioned earlier, I believe "these brothers" refers not only to the 144,000 Jewish evangelists turned loose during the Tribulation, but also to all the surviving Jewish remnant who believe.

Jesus calls these Gentile believers and benevolent helpers **"the righteous"** and **"sheep,"** and invites them into the Kingdom of God as mortal beings. Along with the 144,000 Jewish evangelists, these will be the only mortal (unglorified) persons to live on earth during the thousand-year Kingdom period. They will repopulate the earth.

The **"goats"** are those kings, captains, mighty men and slaves who opposed the returning Christ and persecuted His evangelists. They are now judged and sentenced to eternal fire and then slain with the sword of the Lord. For the next thousand years they suffer in a place called "torments" (Luke 16:19-31). Then, at the time of the Great White Throne Judgment at the end of the Millennium, their bodies are resurrected and after personal judgment they are cast into the Lake of Fire.

Notice that the carnage of men and beasts is so great that God calls forth all the vultures in the air to come and dine at this revolting supper. Too bad. All those judged had the same opportunity as the saints to live in the Kingdom to come. And what a kingdom they missed! Make sure you don't. Stay tuned!

A THOUSAND YEARS OF HEAVEN ON EARTH

CHAPTER THIRTEEN

"Then I, John, saw the holy city, New Jerusalem, coming down out of heaven from God, prepared as a bride adorned for her husband."

—Revelation 21:2

The signs of the times are all around us. I've been chronicling them for 30 years and I really don't think there's any doubt about where this old world is heading in the next few years. Just look at the planet. The earth's ecosystems are breaking down just as the Bible predicted they would. But, even more significantly, man's moral ecosystems are eroding—a sure sign judgment is near.

With chaos, violence and sickness all around us, it's understandable that we would be preoccupied with what's going to happen in the next few years. And, as we've seen thus far in John's Apocalyptic record, it's not a pretty sight. But now it's time to imagine something better—something truly glorious, a time period Christians don't spend nearly enough time contemplating. I'm talking about a future age in which the earth will be restored, when disease will be virtually eliminated, when men's hearts will be healed, when not only the length of our lives will be increased but the quality as well.

Believers often focus so much attention on the Tribulation events leading up to Christ's return that we overlook or misunderstand the volumes of biblical references to the most exciting, glorious and fulfilling time in man's history. That's right. I'm talking about the Millennium.

As we approach the new millennium, people all over the world are fixated once again on the subject of prophecy. At least an equal number of others, unfortunately, are caught up in superstition and deception. But even the believers know very little about the 1000-year period that follows the return of Jesus Christ to planet earth.

Maybe today's believers don't think much about the Millennium because they are under the mistaken impression that they won't really participate in it. On the contrary, we will witness it and be a part of it in a unique way. Let me explain.

THE RAPTURE

I have good news for those of you who are troubled by what you have read, thus far, about the end of this age. If you accept Jesus into your heart and turn your life over to Him now, you won't experience any of these horrors! None! Nada! Zilch! In fact, I believe those of us who do that in this generation will get a special reward.

It's described in I Thessalonians 4:16-17: **"For the**

Lord Himself will descend from heaven with a shout, with the voice of an archangel, and with the trumpet of God. And the dead in Christ will rise first. Then we who are alive and remain shall be caught up together with them in the clouds to meet the Lord in the air. And thus we shall always be with the Lord."

We read about this amazing event again in I Corinthians 15:51-52: "Behold, I tell you a mystery: We shall not all sleep, but we shall all be changed—in a moment, in the twinkling of an eye, at the last trumpet. For the trumpet will sound, and the dead will be raised incorruptible, and we shall be changed."

This is the Rapture. We will discuss it in greater length in the final chapter, but it's important that you understand what will happen to the church just before the beginning of the Tribulation. We're outta here! Isn't that great? So, personally, if you believe in the Lord Jesus Christ with all your heart, you don't have anything to worry about—your fate is sealed. Not only will you live eternally with God, but you will be spared the most torturous time in the history of man.

"So, Hal," you might ask at this point, "if we're raptured out of this world, what will life be like for us during the Millennium?" Good question. Jude 14 teaches that those of us taken out of the world before the Tribulation will return with Jesus when He comes to conquer the earth. In fact, without getting too far ahead of myself, let me just tantalize you by saying that those of us who experience the Rapture will be living in a city hovering above the earthly city of Jerusalem and interacting with the Millennial Kingdom below.

Sound incredible? Well, it's true. That's just what

the opening scripture in this chapter is all about. It's referred to again in Revelation 21:9 and 22:5. This "New Jerusalem"—a city so bright its glow lights the world below by both day and night—is where we will be living in new spiritual bodies that allow us to walk through walls, disappear and reappear at will and travel at the speed of our own desires just as Jesus did in His resurrection body.

So we'll be there—in the Millennial Kingdom—any time we choose. We might visit relatives on earth. We might come down to have a midnight snack. We might even catch a movie, once in a while. But keep in mind, the people down below will be living in their old human bodies—somewhat improved, but not a glorified resurrection body like yours. It will be a very different planet earth than we know today. There will be real justice. Lives will be greatly extended—especially for those who avoid sin and live righteous lives. Satan will be bound in chains during this period. But the world will not be without temptation. Remember, the people of the earth are still human—still living with their sinful nature.

Let's take a look at what John has to say about this fascinating period of history.

"And I saw an angel come down from heaven, having the key of the bottomless pit and a great chain in his hand. And he seized the dragon, that old serpent, who is the Devil and Satan, and bound him a thousand years, and cast him into the bottomless pit, and shut him up, and set a seal upon him, so that he could not deceive the nations anymore, till the thousand years were fulfilled; and after that he must be released a little while.

"And I saw thrones, and they sat upon them, and judgment was given to them; and I saw the souls of those who had been beheaded because of witnessing for Jesus, and standing for the Word of God, who had not worshiped the beast, or his image, or received his mark upon their foreheads, or in their hands; and they lived and reigned [on earth] with Christ a thousand years.

"But the rest of the dead did not live again until the thousand years were finished. This is the first resurrection. Blessed and holy is he who has part in the first resurrection; over these the second death has no power, but they shall be priests of God and of Christ, and shall reign with Him a thousand years.

"And when the thousand years come to an end, Satan shall be loosed out of his prison, and shall go out to deceive the nations which are in the four quarters of the earth, Gog and Magog, to gather them together to battle; the number of whom is as the sand of the seas. And they went out onto the broad expanse of the earth, and surrounded the camp of the saints, and the beloved city; and fire came down from God out of heaven, and devoured them.

"And the Devil who deceived them was cast into the Lake of Fire and brimstone, where the beast and False Prophet are, and shall be tormented day and night forever and ever" (Revelation 20:1-10).

Not surprisingly, there is some theological dispute about this chapter. It centers around whether there will be a literal 1,000-year period of history during which mortal and immortal men will live together in an earthly kingdom ruled by Jesus. The real issue is whether God ever promised such a kingdom, and, if he did, will He keep His promise.

Well, guess what? There are more prophecies in the Bible about this period—this kingdom—and its significance to the believing Jew than any other theme in prophecy. The very heart of the Old Testament prophetic message is the coming of the Messiah to set up an earthly kingdom over which He will rule from the throne of David. The only important detail John's Apocalypse adds concerning this prophesied Messianic kingdom is its duration—1,000 years.

Let's examine the three most popular theological interpretations of this kingdom period:

- **Pre-Millennialism:** This is the oldest view, which holds that Christ will literally and bodily return to earth before the 1,000-year kingdom begins. He will set up this kingdom and reign from the throne of David out of a rebuilt city of Jerusalem. At the end of the 1,000 years, Jesus will turn the kingdom over to His Father, at which point it will merge with God's eternal Kingdom.

  There is no question in my mind that the apostles and early Christians expected Jesus to set up this literal, earthly kingdom. In Acts 1:6, just before Jesus ascended into heaven, the disciples asked Him, "Lord, will you at this time restore the Kingdom to Israel?" In His answer, Christ didn't try to set them straight by telling them there wouldn't be an earthly kingdom for Israel. He simply told them that it wasn't for them to know when it would come to pass, for this was something which only God the Father knew.

  And let's look at the Lord's Prayer—the most

commonly recited prayer in Christianity. Remember, Jesus was instructing His followers how to pray. Think about the words: "Thy Kingdom come. Thy will be done on earth as it is in heaven." His will can't be done on earth in the same way it is in heaven until all of Christ's enemies have been subdued.

One of the major tenets of Pre-Millennialism is that conditions on earth are getting worse rather than better, and that the kingdom age can't begin until Christ returns to destroy whose who have led the world into its downward spiral. Is there any doubt in your mind that conditions on earth are getting worse? Maybe you're a Pre-Millennialist, too.

- **A-Millennialism:** This belief teaches that there will be no 1,000-year reign of Christ on earth and no earthly Kingdom of God. According to this view, when Jesus returns to earth, He will take all believers out, condemn all unbelievers and eternity will begin right there and then.

  This view, of course, tends to allegorize all the prophecies about the promised kingdom. It also teaches—dangerously, I believe—that Israel forfeited all God's promises to her because of unbelief, and that the Church will inherit all the promises originally intended for Israel. A-Millennialists teach that the Church is the fulfillment of the millennial kingdom, and that Christ presently reigns through the Church in peace and righteousness. A-Millennialism, I believe, optimistically sees the Church moving triumphantly to victory.

- **Post-Millennialism:** This view teaches that there will be a literal 1,000 year kingdom on earth, but that Christ will claim His kingdom only after the 1,000 years have expired. Post-Millennialists believe also that the world will get better and better through the spread of the gospel and this will be the millennial age. Then, after the Millennium, Christ will take the believers to heaven and condemn those who reject Him.

My most serious objection to this view is that it teaches that God has finished with Israel as a special nation and people and there is no future for them in this sense. In this view, the Israelites forfeited the unconditional covenants made by a solemn oath of God because of their continued disobedience. To the Pre-Millennialist, this makes God out to be a liar and contradicts clear statements in the New Testament which show the covenants still in force to a believing remnant.

This view also must allegorize most of the New Testament prophetic passages that were fulfilled in 70 AD.

There are countless variations to these three main theological views on the kingdom. But as I study the Scriptures and consider the various views on this question, I'm convinced that the most important issue at stake is that of consistency in Bible interpretation. Most of the prophetic passages can be interpreted in a literal sense as the context indicates they should be.

For instance, in chapter 20 of Revelation, there is absolutely no basis for saying that the narrative should be taken non-literally. There's no way it could have been written more forcefully as objective, future, historical fact, rather than subjective allegory. By the same principle of interpretation which the A-Millennialist uses to make the 1,000-year Kingdom non-literal, I could say that the last judgment isn't literal either. But there's an obvious danger in this: how can you interpret a passage non-literally when there's no evidence of allegory in the passage? Your only authority for doing this is your personal, subjective opinion of God's truth or a deeply ingrained tradition of theology that can be forced on the text. This divests Scripture of its objective and evident authority. This highly questionable method of interpretation has led some people down the primrose path either to liberal theology or to some other form of heresy.

THY KINGDOM COME

The kingdom which Christ will bring and reign over will be a world marvelously beyond man's wildest dreams. John, in his vision in Revelation, doesn't give us many details about this kingdom. He merely emphasizes the fact and duration of it. It's the Old Testament prophets who paint the picture that has whetted the appetite of every heaven-bound traveler for centuries.

They tell us of a kingdom where there will be peace and tranquility, where men will **"beat their swords into plowshares and spears into pruning hooks and learn war no more"** (Isaiah 2:4). This is the world in which the lion will lie down with the lamb, and a man will be a child when he's 100 years old. There will be justice for all. The wicked will be immediately punished. The whole world will be filled with the knowledge of God. Jesus Himself will rule from the capital city, Jerusalem, and there will be a perfect, one-world government.

For man to inhabit the ravaged earth during the Millennium, it will first have to be restored by Jesus. That means the animal and vegetable worlds will be at their highest state of development. The sky will be bluer, the grass will be greener, the flowers will smell sweeter, the air will be cleaner and man will be happier than he ever dreamed possible.

But let's take a look at what John tells us about this period. There are four important phases of the Millennium described in Chapter 20. First, he tells us about a powerful force who comes down from heaven with a most unusual key and chain. He heads straight for Satan and does six things to him: (1) he lays hold on him; (2) he ties him up for 1,000 years; (3) he casts him into a place called the bottomless pit or abyss; (4) he uses the key to lock him up; (5) he sets a seal on him that keeps him from continuing to deceive the nations; and (6) he lets him loose after the 1,000-year period is up.

Although many religions promise their followers a resurrection, they generally have in mind a spiritual resurrection—something that lets the spirit of the person live on in some way but leaves the body to decay and return to dust, never to live again.

Not so with the Judeo-Christian teaching. Both the Old and New Testaments speak of a bodily resurrection of the righteous and unrighteous dead. Four thousand years ago, Job, God's suffering servant, said, **"I know that my Redeemer lives, and that He shall stand in the latter day upon the earth; and after my skin has been destroyed, yet in my flesh I shall see God"** (Job 19:25-26).

In the New Testament, the word resurrection is used about 40 times and almost always speaks of a bodily resurrection. Paul and Peter speak of it with certainty, and Jesus Himself made the strongest statement about it: **"Marvel not at this, for the hour is coming in which all that are in the grave will hear His voice and will come forth"** (John 5:28)

In this chapter of Revelation a First and a Second Resurrection are mentioned. The first one has several phases to it, and is made up of believers only. The Second Resurrection is at the end of the Millennium and is for unbelievers. It is known as "the Resurrection of Condemnation."

Let's examine the four phases of the First Resurrection, the Resurrection of Life. I Corinthians 15:20-25 tells us that Christ was the **"first fruits of the resurrection."** The word **"first fruits"** is taken from the feasts of the Nation of Israel, and means that since Christ was the first man to be permanently raised from the dead, with a body that could never see death, destruction, or decay, we can be assured that others will follow and be resurrected in the same way. Jesus' resurrection was the first phase of the "First Resurrection" mentioned in Revelation 20.

The second phase of this First Resurrection takes place when the Church is caught up at the Rapture. In this stage all the deceased believers who have trusted in Christ from the day of Pentecost until the Rapture will be bodily taken into heaven. The living believers will be snatched up to meet the resurrected Church saints and will be instantaneously transformed from mortal to immortal.

Old Testament believers, however, will not be bodily resurrected until the third phase of the Resurrection. This will take place after the Tribulation, when Christ returns to the earth. At this point all the Old Testament saints and all the martyred Tribulation believers will have their bodies brought out of the grave and united with their souls and spirits. They will receive immortal, eternal bodies and go right into the kingdom (see Daniel 12:1-3).

The mortal believers will live through the 1,000-year Millennial Kingdom will be the final ones to receive eternal bodies by translation. These make up the fourth phase of the first resurrection, which is also called "the resurrection of life." Apparently there will be no death for believers during the kingdom, though there will be the immediate judgment of death for unbelievers if they persist in serious sins.

SATAN UNBOUND AND JUDGED

The Millennial Kingdom will begin with believers only. But apparently many of the children born during this period will not truly accept Jesus as their Savior. Ultimately, they will be deceived by Satan after he is loosed.

Even though there will be great security, equality, prosperity and peace, there will still be those who reject Christ and His forgiveness and secretly harbor rebellion in their hearts. Is that inconceivable? It shouldn't be. Remember that the first rebellion against God started in heaven.

The first thing Satan does when he is released from the abyss is to organize a war. War is one of his favorite enterprises. He gets together some of the descendants of the enemies of Israel who were born during the Millennium, and surrounds Jerusalem. But the rebellion doesn't go far. God zaps them all with fire from heaven and they are annihilated.

This tempest in a teapot is the final curtain call for the Devil. God casts him into the Lake of Fire where he will be tormented forever. I'm sure this doesn't bring any joy to God's heart. Remember, this creature, Lucifer, was once God's most beautiful and intelligent creation. Yet, in light of all the suffering he has caused, it's time for great thanksgiving. I'm sure the universe breathes a collective sigh of relief when he's finally put away for good.

What about the fourth phase of the Resurrection? That comes in the next part of this chapter of Revelation, which explains the last judgment and the mystery of the books.

THE RESURRECTION OF DAMNATION

CHAPTER FOURTEEN

"Blessed and holy is the one who has a part in
the First Resurrection; over these the second
death has no power...And those whose bodies
had been raised (in the Second Resurrection)
from death and Hades were thrown into the
Lake of fire. This is the Second Death,
the Lake of fire."

—The Apocalypse 20:6 &14

SOME AMAZING MISCONCEPTIONS ABOUT FINAL JUDGMENT

He who is born but once
Shall die twice;
But he who is born twice
Shall die but once."
—Hal Lindsey

always have a heavy heart when I approach this
preview of the Last Judgment and the final dispo-
sition of every person who did not receive God's
free pardon. Down through history the Last
Judgement has been a subject of interest to secular

philosophers, writers and even great artists like Michelangelo. Yet most reflect very erroneous ideas about this ultra-important subject.

The most popular misconception is that all mankind will find out their final status in eternity at one great last judgment. This popular misconception also teaches that at this judgment our good deeds will be weighed against our bad to decide whether we are worthy for eternal life with God. If not, we are either cast into a temporary place of torment called purgatory, where a person suffers to pay off the debt of his sins for a few hundred years, or in some extreme cases, a person is just sent straight to hell. This is not even close to what the Bible teaches. There are a number of judgments taught in the Bible that occur at different times in history. Here are the judgments in order:

NO. 1: THE CROSS, GOD'S JUDGMENT AGAINST THE SINS OF THE WORLD

The first and most important judgment took place at the cross. It was there that God dealt with the sin problem, to remove it forever as a barrier between Him and mankind. This is why God, the second person, stepped out of eternity and took on the nature of a true man in the person of Jesus.

This unique man was born of a human mother, but God Himself was the Father of this child. This is why the man, Jesus of Nazareth, is called the Son of God in a sense no one else can ever be—because God alone is His Father. The Angel explained this to Mary when she asked how she, a virgin, could bear a son: **"The Holy Spirit will come upon you, and the power of the Most High will overshadow you; and for that** reason **THE HOLY OFFSPRING shall be called the Son of God"** (Luke 1:35 NASB). Note carefully, it is the holy offspring that is called **the Son of God,** not the eternal second person of the Godhead who permanently joined his divine nature with this sinless human nature. From Bethlehem onward, this unique person chose not to use his divine nature, but to voluntarily act only through his human nature. This was necessary in order to qualify as a true human being. For only a true man who had no sin of his own could qualify to die for the sins of mankind.

If Jesus had been born of a human father, He would have had the sin of Adam passed down to him, because the legal culpability for the first sin is passed down through the man, not the woman. This is explained by the Apostle, **"And it was not Adam who was deceived, but the woman being quite deceived fell into transgression"** (1 Timothy 2:14). **"So then as through one transgression** [Adam] **there result-ed condemnation to all men, even so through one act of righteousness** [Jesus' sacrifice for our sins on the cross] **there resulted justification of life to all men"** (Romans 5:18). This is why the virgin birth was absolutely necessary. Jesus had to be without inherited sin, as well as without personal sin, in order to qualify to die in our place and purchase a pardon for all mankind.

The great judgment for the sins of all mankind took place when Jesus the Messiah willingly took our sins upon Himself and then bore the full measure of God's holy judgment against us. This is stated clearly by Paul, **"...God was in Christ reconciling the world to Himself, not counting their trespasses against them...He made Him to be sin on our behalf, that** we might become the righteousness of God in Him" (2 Corinthians 5:19, 21). By His death in our place, He removed sin as a barrier. Now God has set Himself free to reach out to us and say, "Only believe in My Son and what He did for you, receive the pardon He purchased for you, and you now have forgiveness for all sins and eternal life with me."

Therefore, since judgment for sins has already taken place, all who believe in Jesus Christ will never stand at a judgment of condemnation—because the believer has already been judged and pardoned at the Cross.

NO. 2: THE JUDGEMENT OF THE BELIEVERS TO DETERMINE REWARDS.

Only believers will stand at this judgment. This takes place after the Rapture and resurrection of all believers from the Church Age. This is called **the Judgment Seat of Christ.**

The Bible says about this, **"Each man's work will become evident; for the day will show it, because it is to be revealed with fire; and the fire itself will test the quality of each man's work. If any man's work remains, he shall receive a reward. If any man's work is burned up, he will suffer loss; but HE HIMSELF SHALL BE SAVED, yet so as through fire"** (1 Corinthians 3:13-15).

All who stand at this judgment are saved—not one is lost or condemned. They simply learn whether the works they did as a Christian were done with the right motive through faith, or whether they lose rewards.

NO. 3: THE JUDGMENT OF SURVIVORS OF THE TRIBULATION

This takes place immediately at the Second Coming of the Messiah Jesus. Both believers and non-believers are gathered together before the Lord Jesus and He separates the believers from the unbelievers. The illustration of a shepherd separating sheep from goats is used by Jesus. The believers are sent into the Messianic Kingdom as mortals to repopulate the earth and serve under Jesus, who will rule the world from the dynasty or throne of His royal lineage from King David. The nonbelievers are cast into the place known as Hades, or Hell, to await the Last Judgment.

NO. 4: JUDGMENT OF THE OLD TESTAMENT & TRIBULATION BELIEVERS

This takes place at the time of the Second Coming also. The prophet Daniel predicted this: **"...And at that time your people, EVERYONE WRITTEN IN THE BOOK, will be rescued. And many of those who sleep in the dust of the ground will awake, these to everlasting life..."** (Daniel 12:1-2). Also see the Apocalypse (20:4-5), which speaks of the resurrection of the martyrs from the Tribulation.

NO. 5: THE LAST JUDGMENT OF THE GREAT WHITE THRONE

This is a judgment for unbelievers of all time. The Second Resurrection is also called the Resurrection of Condemnation. It brings back unbelievers, both in body and soul form, who were contained in places called death and hades.

The horror of it all is that everyone who is raised from the dead by the Second Resurrection is condemned—without exception—to the most terrible condition and place imaginable. It is called the **"Second Death"**, which is **"the Lake of Fire"** that burns forever. In this second resurrection, all mankind that did not accept the free gift of pardon provided by Jesus Christ must answer for their choice.

The really tough question to answer in the light of this is, "Since everyone who stands at this judgment will be condemned; and since The Lord declared that those who do not believe in Him have been condemned already, what is the point of the Great White Throne? What more can be said if the case has already been decided?

"And I saw a Great White Throne, and Him who sat on it, from whose face the earth and the heaven fled away, and there was found no place for them. And I saw the dead, small and great, stand before God, and THE BOOKS were opened; and ANOTHER BOOK was opened, which is the Book of Life. And the dead were judged out of those things which were written in the books, according to their works. And the sea gave up the dead that were in it, and death and hades delivered up the dead that were in them; and they were judged every man according to their works. And those from death and hades were cast into the Lake of Fire. This is the second death. And whoever was not found written in the Book of Life was cast into the Lake of Fire" (Revelation 20:11-15).

WHY A FINAL JUDGMENT?

The one sin for which Jesus could not pay is the sin of rejecting the free pardon for which He paid with His life. This one unpardonable sin that sends a person to eternal separation from God in the Lake of Fire is reported by the Apostle John from Jesus' own words, **"He who believes in Him is not judged; he who does not believe has been judged already, because he has not believed in the name of the only begotten Son of God"** (John 3:18). The only issue is whether a person has believed in Jesus as his pardon for sin, or not. It doesn't matter what denomination a person may be from. That has nothing to do with the salvation of a person. So the unbeliever doesn't have to wait for Judgment to know whether he is one of the saved. He is already judged and lost. If he continues till death in this stance, there is no more chance to change his status.

The obvious question arises: If the unbeliever is already condemned, what is the purpose of the last judgment at the Great White Throne of God? The purpose of this final confrontation between God and unbelieving man is clearly to demonstrate to the unbeliever why he is already condemned. God will hold up the works that the unbeliever thought were good enough when added to his sincerity. God will take the best works that the unbeliever has done and hold them up against His righteousness and not one will be good enough. So the unbeliever will finally have to confess that no one is good enough and that he is rightly condemned for only one reason: not his personal sins—Jesus died and paid for them. The one sin that is sending the unbeliever to hell is his rejection of the gift of pardon that Jesus died to make free to him.

This is what Jesus meant when He predicted the special work the Holy Spirit would do to make us effective evangelists. Jesus said that the Holy Spirit would convict the whole world **"of sin, because they do not believe in Me"** (John 16:9). You see, the Holy Spirit only convicts the unbeliever of the one sin that will send him to hell. Because it isn't his sins, plural, that will send him there.

THE MYSTERY OF THE BOOKS

In chapter 20, verse 12, John tells us that the books were opened, including one called **"the Book of Life."** All unbelievers are judged from these books. But what are these books?

I believe the first book opened will be the **"Book of God's Law."** In numerous verses in the Bible, God's written Word is referred to as the **"Book of the Law."** We're told that anyone who has had exposure to God's Word is responsible to live accordingly. If not, he's condemned on the basis of the Law.

No doubt there will be many standing before God who can honestly plead that their ears had never heard one word from God's law in their lifetime. To them God will affirm what He inspired the Apostle Paul to write to the early Church, namely, that those who have not heard the Law have had it written instinctively in their consciences by God Himself. Their conscience will be the standard by which they are condemned, because they haven't always lived up to the good which their consciences showed them.

THE BOOK OF WORKS

The second book which will be opened is the **"Book of Works."** Evidently each person has a recording angel who is writing down all of his works. Every time he has an opportunity to receive Christ as Savior and turns it down, it's recorded in the book. Every bad deed as well as every good deed that's been done with the wrong motivation is also written down and will be brought up to the doer.

If you've received the forgiveness that God offers in His Son's death for you, then God has already judged all the wrong things you've done or will do; Jesus has already taken God's wrath against those sins in your behalf. The believer is already accepted with God on the basis of Jesus Christ's merits. You don't have to worry that God will keep a list of all your evil deeds and hold them against you. He nailed your list to the Cross, and Jesus buried it in the grave. And you will not be here.

But even though God has recorded all the works that we would consider bad, they will not be the basis for our condemnation. No, it's the things we did that we thought were good and should earn us acceptance with God that will be brought up. God will prove to every person who stands at the last judgment that, compared to His righteousness, **"We are all as an unclean thing, and all our good deeds are as filthy rags in His sight"** (Isaiah 64:6).

God's only way of salvation is revealed in these two verses: **"For by grace you have been saved through faith, and that not of yourself; it is the gift of God, not of works, so no man can boast"** (Ephesians 2:8 and 9).

THE BOOK OF LIFE

The last book to witness against those awaiting their sentences at God's throne is the **"Book of Life."** The New Testament refers to the **"Book of Life"** eight times. The Old Testament doesn't reference it by name, but it does refer three times to a book in which names are written. This book contained the names, before the foundation of the earth, of every person who would ever be born. When a person either makes a decision that God knows has hardened his heart forever, or dies without receiving God's free pardon, **then his name is blotted out of the Book of Life.** At the end of time, this Book will have remaining only the names of the believers.

In contrast to this, a person's name is entered into the **Lamb's Book of Life** WHEN he believes. So God has a double bookkeeping system that prevents any possibility of error. At the last Judgment, both Books of Life will contain only the believers' names.

THE GREATEST TRAGEDY

To me, life's greatest tragedy is to watch an unbeliever die, leaving unused and canceled a full Pardon for all his sins that had his name on it. The realization of such a thing will torment the unbeliever for all eternity when he reviews time and time again that he could have believed but instead rejected it...In God's estimation, he has literally scoffed at the blood of the Son of God and counted it as unworthy of him.

Don't let this become your tragic story. Receive your gift of pardon and invite the Lord Jesus into your life. According to God's own solemn promise, you are forgiven all sins past, present and future at this point.

The Holy Spirit imparts to you a new spiritual life that gives you the capacity to understand God's Word and His ways. The Holy Spirit also takes up permanent residence in you to guide and aid you through this life in a productive and fulfilling way that pleases God. He also develops the spiritual gifts that are given you at your spiritual birth so that you become uniquely equipped to fulfill His will for your life. Begin that great adventure today!

CHAPTER FIFTEEN

THOU SHALT NOT SWEAT IT!

CHAPTER FIFTEEN

"This is what the Lord says to you: 'Do not be afraid or discouraged because of this vast army. For the battle is not yours, but God's...You will not have to fight this battle.'"

— II Chronicles 20:15,17

If we are indeed living in the last days of God's prophetic program before the return of Jesus Christ to redeem the planet, then the early part of the 21st century is going to be a frightful time for the world. The preceding chapters have laid out a grim scenario of death, destruction and disease of heretofore unimaginable proportions. Many of us can already see the early signs of the trends and conditions that will worsen in the period of the Tribulation—making life on earth a living hell for billions. I believe the Bible is clear in showing us that Christians will not be immune to some suffering before this seven-year period begins.

So what should we do? How should we respond? How can we prepare ourselves? First of all, let me say that we should not be afraid of these times. As I have said so often, I would rather be alive right now than at any other time in history. Some Christians might argue that being alive during Christ's earthly ministry would have been a great blessing—and indeed it would have been.

Yet, I believe this generation of believers has an opportunity to be blessed even more. For we are the generation that is going to see the sudden rending of the clouds and hear the Son of God shout, "Come up here!" Before the sound is fully comprehended, we will be in the presence of our Great God and Savior, Jesus the Messiah. Without experiencing death, we will have eternal glorified bodies exactly like His. I will discuss this event in more detail in the last chapter.

But that is not the only reason I'm so excited to be alive now. You see, God loves us with an intense and personal touch. He will never allow any of us to be tested beyond what we are able to bear. Not all of us may experience the coming persecutions and trials, but we all need to learn how to appropriate God's provisions for daily living. We all need to arm ourselves spiritually—to become skilled in using the special protections and defenses God provides for us.

It's not a question of *if* we are going to go through trials in our lives. It's a question of *when*. And there is not a doubt in my mind that all believers will be faced with more trials and more severe tests in the coming years. It's simply a sign of the times. So let's examine the antidote He has provided for each and every one of us.

God promises an experience of perfect inner peace in spite of the coming adversities—an experience of joy and inner happiness that continues no matter how difficult and unpleasant our situation becomes. He promises an experience of spiritual stamina and courage, no matter how intense and frightening our circumstances may be. He promises an experience of unshakable hope and stability when our world and all that is familiar is falling apart. He promises an experience of power when all of our human strength is depleted. And He promises an experience of wisdom and confidence when we need to stand up proudly for the truth and authenticity of the Word of God.

This may all sound like hocus-pocus to you. You've already been in situations where you were uncertain—even fearful. You never got that reassurance. Maybe you consider yourself a spiritual failure. Maybe you've tried to be a believer and never felt empowered by the Holy Spirit. Perhaps you have never opened your heart fully to God but find yourself troubled by what you see happening in the world around you.

Know this: His peace in the midst of the storm can be your daily experience. I feel so sorry for people who don't know God—who don't understand His promises and what He has to offer us, not only in the next life, but in this one. I think about cult members so lost they take their own lives—the most precious gift God can give—in an effort to find meaning. I think about how many opportunities people in our society have to know God through His Word while others throughout the world have been systematically denied this chance. I think about the way so many in the world who have heard the truth have found themselves denying it and worshipping false gods—from government to money to hollow idols.

Maybe you think you're unworthy. Well, you're not alone. We are all unworthy. That's the point. But God delights in taking the least likely candidates and turning them into mighty men and women of faith. God, Who cannot lie, has promised all of these things to those who simply claim them by faith—a faith that is hardly irrational, but built upon the thousands of promises made and kept by God throughout the last 5,000 years of recorded history.

FAITH IS THE KEY

Faith is the key to all these provisions. With this special brand of "last days" faith—what I have called "Combat Faith"—we learn to believe the promises of God in spite of our emotions, our feelings or circumstances. It is a faith that has been trained in the crucible of the trials so that it keeps on believing when the going gets tough.

Few subjects in the Bible are more important for us to understand than that of faith. Here are just a few of the things that the Bible declares to come through faith:

- We are born into eternal life through faith.
- We are declared righteous before God by faith.
- We are forgiven by faith.
- We are healed by faith.
- We understand the mysteries of creation by faith.
- We learn God's Word by faith.
- By faith we understand things to come.
- We walk by faith and not by sight.
- We overcome the world by faith.
- We enter God's rest by faith.
- We are controlled and empowered by the Holy Spirit by faith.

- We can please God only by faith.
- Everything we try to do for God that is not rooted in faith is sin.

In short, the issue of faith pervades every aspect of our relationship with God and our service for Him. Faith is the source of our strength, our provision, our courage, our guidance and our victory over the world, the flesh and the Devil. Faith is the only thing that can sustain us in the trials and persecutions predicted for the last days.

It is therefore imperative that we understand exactly what faith is, how we get it and how it grows. For the Christian, no other pursuit is as urgent as the quest for faith. This has always been true, but in the light of the prophetic signs that herald Jesus' soon return and the inevitable perilous times that precede His coming, it is even more urgent today.

THE DEFINITION OF FAITH

Like so many other things, faith is hard to define. Even the Bible does not offer a concise definition—but I believe the closest Scripture comes is in Hebrews 11:1: **"Now faith is being sure of what we hope for and certain of what we do not see."** Think about that. Faith has two dimensions—the future and the present unseen spiritual world. True faith enables us to perceive the invisible spiritual world about us, and to operate with confidence in this intangible dimension.

All of God's miraculous power flows through the believer who enters into God's supernatural dimension described in this promise: **"For the one who has entered His rest has himself also rested from his works, as God did from His"** (Hebrews 4:10 NASB). It is from this dynamic base called God's rest, which is entered by faith, that all divinely approved living must flow. The faith-rest might be called God's twelfth commandment: "Thou shalt not sweat it!" (The eleventh being "Love one another as I have loved you.")

The Holy Spirit introduces us to that experience called "God's rest," according to Scripture. Let's look at the book of Hebrews, verses 3:7–4:11 (NASB) to get a better picture:

"Therefore, just as the Holy Spirit says,
'Today if you hear His voice,
Do not harden your hearts as when they provoked Me,
As in the day of trial in the wilderness,
Where your fathers tried Me by testing Me,
And saw My works for forty years.
Therefore I was angry with this generation,
And said, "They always go astray in their heart;
And they did not know My ways; "As I swore as in My wrath,
"They shall not enter My rest." '

"Take care, brethren, lest there should be in any one of you an evil, unbelieving heart, in falling away from the living God. But encourage one another day after day, as long as it is still called 'Today,' lest any one of you be hardened by the deceitfulness of sin. For we have become partakers of [partners with] Christ, if we hold fast the beginning of our assurance firm until the end; while it is said, 'Today if you hear His voice, Do not harden your hearts, as when they provoked Me.'

"For who provoked Him when they had heard? Indeed, did not all those who came out of

Egypt led by Moses? And with whom was He angry for forty years? Was it not with those who sinned, whose bodies fell in the wilderness? And to whom did He swear that they should not enter His rest, but to those who were so disobedient? And so we see that they were not able to enter because of unbelief.

"Therefore, let us fear lest, while a promise remains of entering His rest, any one of you should seem to have come short of it. For indeed we have had good news preached to us, just as they also did; but the word they heard did not profit them, because it was not united by faith in those who heard. For we who have believed enter that rest, just as He has said, 'As I swore in My wrath, They shall not enter My rest,' although His works were finished from the foundation of the world. For He has thus said somewhere concerning the seventh day, 'And God rested on the seventh day from all His works'; and again in this passage, 'They shall not enter My rest.'

"Since therefore it remains for some to enter it, and those who formerly had good news preached to them failed to enter because of disobedience, He again fixes a certain day, 'Today,' saying through David after so long a time just as has been said before, 'Today if you hear His voice, Do not harden your hearts.' For if Joshua had given them rest, He would not have spoken of another day after that.

"There remains therefore a Sabbath rest for the people of God. For the one who has entered His rest has himself also rested from his works, as God did from His.

"Let us therefore be diligent to enter that rest, lest anyone fall through following the same example of disobedience."

The main message of this passage is that we must enter this state called "God's rest." There is an urgency to it. It is not something that can be put off. The way you enter that state is by believing His promises.

THE MEANING OF GOD'S REST

Some interpreters of this passage in Hebrews have suggested that it is an illustration of entering salvation through faith in Christ. But in the context of this passage, entering the promised land of Canaan is a picture of God's people entering His rest and conquering through faith. If entering the promised land and God's rest were a picture of entering salvation, then even Moses and Aaron were not saved, because they were not allowed to enter the land. Of all that generation, only Joshua and Caleb were allowed to enter the promised land.

The Passover and Red Sea deliverance were divine symbols of salvation. When Israel entered the promised land, they took possession of it by means of war. Though they pursued their enemies with drawn sword, they rested by faith in the promises of God.

This is the picture that God draws to illustrate His rest and how to live the Christian life today. Though we are in the midst of a great spiritual war, we can rest inwardly and have perfect peace. The Holy Spirit clothes Himself with the one who believes God's promises, and then works through him.

THE BEGINNING OF SORROWS

All suffering directly or indirectly comes as an inevitable consequence of man's original rejection of God and the loss of relationship with Him. Mankind was originally created perfect and was placed in a paradise where his every conceivable need was provided. He had a relationship with God and was designed to find fulfillment and function properly, only through fellowship with Him.

For this reason, man was created in the image of God. He had will, intellect, emotion, moral reason and everlasting existence. All of these attributes have to do with his immaterial being—or soul.

Man was given will so that he could choose to love God and have fellowship with Him. He was given intellect so that he could understand God's revelation to Him. He was given emotion so that he could respond to God's love. But the risk was that man could reject his relationship with God and go his own way into destruction. The very attributes that give man the capacity for relationship and fellowship with God also give him the capacity for great evil.

LIFE IS A TRAINING GROUND

Isn't it exciting to know that every decision we make in our lives has eternal repercussions? Everything we do in this life—every act of obedience, every act of faith, every trial endured—is significant and can earn us eternal rewards. Nothing is without meaning.

In a very real sense, this life is a training ground for the next. We are being prepared for an eternal mission in our Heavenly Father's infinite universe. The way we respond to our opportunities to believe the Lord now, qualifies us for our future position and role in His kingdom.

The rewards we'll get in the future are of a magnitude so much greater than the tiny dimensions of our faithful services in the present that they defy human comprehension. Note the superlatives God uses in comparing our present labors with our future rewards and glory: **"For momentary, light affliction is producing for us an eternal weight of glory far beyond all comparison, while we look not at the things which are seen...for the things which are seen are temporal, but the things which are not seen are eternal"** (II Corinthians 4:17-18 NASB).

Isn't it interesting that Paul kept focusing on things that are not visible. This is the secret of endurance in our battles of faith and the way to win the victory. Jesus has already won the war. By trusting and resting in Him, we enter His victory in our battles.

Thus, no matter how bad things get—or seem to get—there is never any need to lose heart or be discouraged. Even as our physical bodies deteriorate with age, our inner spiritual strength is renewed day by day. What's the worst thing that can happen to us in this life? We die—physically. But what a comfort knowing that death will bring us closer to a relationship with God and to an eternal life far better than anything we could ever imagine!

And, what's more, many of us in this generation will not even have to know physical death. So, remember the 12th commandment: "Thou shalt not sweat it."

PREPARE FOR LIFTOFF

CHAPTER SIXTEEN

"Behold I tell you a mystery; we shall not all sleep [die], but we shall all be changed."

—I Corinthians 15:51

It breaks my heart as I watch the evening news and pore over the daily newspaper and see how rapidly the world as we know it is moving toward catastrophe—the kind of bone-chilling economic, political, environmental and spiritual disasters I have described in this book. Think about the world around us:

- **Russia,** a declining superpower with one of the world's largest nuclear stockpiles, and China, a rising economic behemoth with a growing arsenal, have teamed up to form what they call a "strategic partnership" for the 21st century, reminding those familiar with biblical prophecy that these two

PREPARE FOR LIFTOFF **295**

nations will be involved in invasions of the Middle East during the last great war on Earth.

- **China** now maintains the largest standing army in the world with nearly 3 million in active service. But add to that the number of militiamen under arms and you have an armed force of more than 200 million—the size of the army prophesied in the Apocalypse. China's rise to economic super-power status continues on overdrive and will be propelled faster and further by its annexing of Hong Kong. Already the second-largest economy in the world with a gross domestic product of $3,500 billion, China's double-digit growth will place it on a par with the U.S.'s $7,248 billion sometime early in the next decade.

- **Christians** are already the most persecuted religious group in the world today, according to the international human rights group Freedom House. Eleven countries now practice systematic persecution of Christians, says Nina Shea, author of *In the Lion's Den.* They are China, Pakistan, Laos, North Korea, Vietnam, Cuba, Saudi Arabia, Sudan, Egypt, Nigeria and Uzbekistan. These 11 nations—and others that practice a more random brand of persecution—are dominated by one of two belief systems, Communism or militant Islam.

- **Infectious diseases** have increased in the United States by 58 percent since 1980, according to the latest data. While much of that increase can be attributed to the AIDS virus, more people also are dying of common infections like pneumonia. The increase also reflects the emergence of virulent new infections, the re-emergence of nasty old ones and growing resistance to antibiotics. As grave as the situation is in the United States, it is far worse throughout the rest of the world. Global incidences of cholera, tuberculosis, diphtheria and bubonic plague have all increased dramatically in the past five years. The mosquito-borne illness dengue, which produces deadly fevers, has shown up in Latin America and the Caribbean for the first time in more than 20 years. Meanwhile, the World Health Organization says bacteria resistant to common antibiotics represent the most serious threat to the global medical community for the foreseeable future.

- **Unpredictable**—and often deadly—weather has the most serious climate researchers in the world wondering what's going on. Is it global warming? Is it ozone depletion? Is it something we just don't understand? "After the mid-1970s, suddenly everything started looking really erratic," explains Nick Graham, a climate researcher at the Scripps Institute of Oceanography in La Jolla, Calif. "Everything changed here. We had dry falls. We had winters that were wetter. And it wasn't just here, it was climate change all over the world."

- **Earthquakes** continue to increase in frequency and intensity, just as the Bible predicts for the last days before the return of Christ. History shows that the number of killer quakes remained fairly constant until the 1950s—averaging between two to four per decade. In the 1950s, there were nine. In the 1960s, there were 13. In the 1970s, there were 51. In the 1980s, there were 86. From 1990 through 1996, there have been more than 150.

- **The United Nations** Environment Program reports that plants, animals and entire ecosystems are threatened at much higher rates than ever before in recorded history. At least 4,000 plants and 5,400 animals are threatened with extinction, according to the latest assessment. In addition, species are becoming extinct at a rate 50 to 100 times higher than normal.

- For years I have been telling people to keep their eyes on **Turkey**—a strategically important nation and one whose prophetic significance is sometimes underrated. Recently, Ankara has been cozying up to Iran and Iraq, including the striking of a multibillion-dollar natural gas deal with Iran, defying a threat of U.S. anti-terrorist sanctions. Immediately after signing the deal, Turkish officials visited Baghdad seeking to improve relations with Iraq. The Armageddon coalition described in Ezekiel 38 is well into formation.

- **IBM and a group of 15 U.S. and Canadian banking giants**—including Bank of America, Banc One and Mellon Bank—have entered a joint venture that will greatly expand the world of electronic financial services with a short-term goal of replacing all cash and check transactions with electronic transfers in the very near future. Other banks and companies are moving even faster. Citibank has developed an Electronic Money System that will permit consumers to make payments electronically anywhere in the world. Where is all this leading? *The Philadelphia Inquirer* reported Jan. 21, 1996: "Thirty years from now, chips will be implanted in our bodies encoded with credit card, passport, driver's license and other personal information." Other experts say it won't take that long.

- **The United Religions Summit** is reconvening to write a charter intended to unify the world's faiths. "We are on the threshold of a new global civilization," explained William Swing, a California Episcopal bishop who has spearheaded the movement. "When people look around, religion has just not been at the table." Working hand in hand with Swing is United Nations Assistant Secretary-General Robert Muller, who once wrote: "If Christ came back to earth, his first visit would be to the United Nations to see if his dream of human oneness and brotherhood had come true." Muller, by the way, is associated with the Lucis Trust, a New Age organization that evolved from the Lucis Publishing Company, previously known as the Lucifer Publishing Company. Draw your own conclusions about which master such men serve.

- **Every year since the signing of the Treaty of Rome in 1957,** Europe has become more powerful on the world stage. Beginning with only six member nations—France, Germany, Italy, the Netherlands, Belgium and Luxembourg—it has grown into an economic and political behemoth of 15 nations populated by 360 million with the additions of member-states Britain, Spain, Portugal, Greece, Ireland and Austria. Now there is significant pressure to expand the union. It is from this economic and political colossus that the unholy global ruler will emerge, according to Scripture.

Euthanasia… partial-birth abortions… cloning… cult suicides… UFO sightings… Satanic ritual murders…famines… volcanoes… I could go on and on. But you get the point. To most people, all of this may just sound like a collection of unrelated news. But to the student of prophecy, it all ties together. It's all part of a pattern. It's exactly the kind of developments we would expect to see in the generation that witnessed the rebirth of the nation of Israel and the recapturing of Jerusalem by the Jewish people. They are signs of the times.

Ironically, it's not just Bible prophecy students who see the world moving toward climax. Lots of others agree—from Indian shamen to secular scientists. So what's our hope? Death and resurrection? That is indeed a great hope, but believers of this generation have something else to anticipate—a unique and mysterious experience. I'm talking about something I alluded to earlier—the event known to Bible students as the Rapture. But, first, some background.

OUR RESURRECTION BODIES

In I Corinthians, chapter 15, the Apostle Paul, under the inspiration of God's Holy Spirit, is teaching about the certainty of every believer's resurrection from the dead. He also reveals that the resurrection body will be wonderfully changed into an eternal immortal form that has real corporal substance.

Paul teaches that our new body will **"bear the image of the heavenly,"** that is, it will be like the Lord Jesus' resurrected body. In this regard, he says, **"Flesh and blood cannot inherit the kingdom of God; nor does the perishable inherit the imperishable"** (I Corinthians 15:50).

In other words, our present body of flesh and blood, which must be sustained by elements of the earth which are perishable, must be changed to another form. This new form has material being, but it is of a kind that is suited for the spiritual, imperishable, eternal atmosphere of heaven.

The resurrected Lord Jesus is the measure of our future existence. He could appear and disappear at will. He could move through solid walls. He could be seen and felt. He could eat food, though apparently it wasn't necessary. Though glorified, Jesus could be recognized.

Furthermore, the Bible shows us, our resurrected bodies will no longer experience death, aging, crying, mourning, sorrow or pain. The only problem with resurrection, however, is that you have to die to experience it. But in the midst of Paul's teaching on resurrection, he says, **"Behold, I tell you a mystery; we shall not all sleep, but we shall all be changed"** (I Corinthians 15:51).

What Paul is telling us here is that Christians will not all die. He explains: **"In a moment, in the twinkling of an eye, at the last trumpet; for the trumpet will sound, and the dead will be raised imperishable, and we shall be changed"** (I Corinthians 15:52). Just think of it. In the flash of a nanosecond, every living believer on earth will be gone, vanished, bye-bye, sayonara, outta here. Now this is not good news for those left on earth. Imagine what it will be like when only unbelievers are populating the earth. But God has a plan there, too, as you saw earlier in this book, with regard to the 144,000 Jewish evangelists who will just as suddenly see the light.

As for us, one moment we will be going about our life here on earth, and the next moment we will be hurtled into the presence of Jesus. We'll also get to see our loved ones who have died. It will be a grand reunion all around.

Paul also tells us in I Thessalonians that we will also be reunited with all those we have led to the Lord:

**"For who is our hope or joy or crown of exulta-
tion? Is it not even you, in the presence of our
Lord Jesus at His coming?"** (I Thessalonians: 2:19).

How will all this happen, exactly? Well, we'll literally be **"caught up in the clouds to meet the Lord
in the air,"** according to I Thessalonians 4:17. When
will this happen? In Luke 12, Jesus tells believers to be
ready for His return because He is coming **"at an hour
that you do not expect"** (Luke 12:40).

Now, let me ask you this: If believers were around
to see the emergence of the Antichrist, the invasion of
Israel by Russia and the other major signs of the end
times that occur during the Tribulation period, would
they not be expecting Jesus to come for them at any
moment? Any believer alive at that time would certainly be anticipating this event. Yet Jesus tells us that
He will come for us suddenly and without a specific
warning.

We are snatched away before we even know what
hit us. We are then taken to His Father's House where
He has already prepared a place for us (John 14:1-4). So
the Rapture literally could occur at any moment. It
could happen today. Your reading of this passage may
indeed be God's special way to reach you—before it's
too late.

No one knows the day or the hour. Don't believe
anyone who tells you otherwise. But Jesus did give us
a way of knowing the general times. Just read Luke
21:29-32. Or study the parable of the fig tree in
Matthew 24:32-34.

Jesus tells us clearly that the generation that sees
the beginnings of these signs will see the fulfillment of
all the prophecies leading to the Second Coming. Well,

folks, Israel has been reborn. Jerusalem is under the rulership of the Jews again. We are already experiencing the beginnings of the persecution of the church. False prophets are emerging. Deceiving spirits are leading many astray. The world is headed for global government. Weather patterns are changing. There are plagues and earthquakes and volcanoes. How else can one explain this convergence of activity?

"But, Hal," you might ask at this point, "how can I be sure I will be one of those taken?" You've got to remember that salvation is a gift of God. All you have to do is be willing to accept it and let His Holy Spirit change your life.

I know, I know. You're not ready to change your life. You don't think you can do it. That's not the point. This is not something you can do anyway. Just let God do it. Trust Him. He will change your heart and its desires to conform with His. And He will assure you of eternal life the instant you receive Him and His pardon from sin.

"The one who believes in Me, though he should die, yet shall he live; and the one who lives and believes in Me shall never die."—A promise from Jesus the Messiah (John 11:25).

God bless you one and all!
I'll see you in paradise!

INDEX

VERSE INDEX

**Aging Without
Growing Old**
By Judy Lindberg McFarland

**Happy Days
And Dark Nights**
By Jerry and Susanne
McClain

**Yes Yes Living
In A No No World**
By Neil Eskelin

**What To Do When
You Don't Know
What To Do**
By Neil Eskelin

Available At Your
Local Bookstore